GW00499271

Revival of the Land

CREAG MEAGAIDH
NATIONAL NATURE RESERVE

Revival of the Land – Creag Meagaidh National Nature Reserve is a highly readable account of the regeneration of the natural landscape in a National Nature Reserve.

The story is set in a vividly portrayed historical context, sensitively illustrated by leading wildlife and landscape photographers.

The book describes ten years of innovative deer and forest management and examines the relevance of this approach to other highland estates. In pointing the way to a future for the Highlands in which forestry, wildlife, sport, landscape and people can share the benefits of sustainable practices, the book celebrates a true success story of the highlands.

It is essential reading for landowners, factors and conservationists, and fascinating reading for all those interested in the land.

Revival of the Land

At L-leasachadh an fhearainn

CREAG MEAGAIDH
NATIONAL NATURE RESERVE

by
Paul Ramsay
for Scottish Natural Heritage

SCOTTISH
NATURAL
HERITAGE

L. GILL

An alder tree in open
birch woodland –
vegetative regrowth
follows reduced
browsing pressure.

CONTENTS

FOREWORD

Fionn MacCumhail asked his sons: 'What is the greatest music of all?' The first replied 'The clash of swords in the battle', and the second 'The baying of the hounds at the chase' and the third 'The sound of the harp in the great hall', but their father replied 'No, my sons, the greatest music of all is what is happening'.

That tale would surely be eloquent endorsement of the ten years recorded in this book. Even from my first coming to Laggan almost 50 years ago change was inevitable, but it makes the love of the place no less. Many of the young men had gone away to two wars, which drew a scythe through their ranks, as through the forests planted by Sir John Ramsden to whose grand-daughter I proposed at the top of Coire a' Chriochairein at the time of the roaring. I herded the wethers for Neil Usher on Moy and did his lambing on Aberarder in 1955, after a winter when the snow was blown in five-foot drifts against the windows of the house. There were still wildcats in the rocks of the wood, and badgers, and eight pairs of eagles between Ardverikie, Aberarder and Moy, and a house cow to milk in the byre. A few planks of Magnus's bothy remained – the place of the old deer watcher – and it was still possible to sit there on top of the hill and listen to the golden plover passing as one talked to the wind – then was then, and now is now. The inn at Kinloch Laggan is no longer.

The post office closed with Martha's going. The Highlands and Islands cinema is a distant memory in the hall and now there is no school, but let no-one sneer at the past, for we cared deeply for the land, knowing the ebbing of the soil's fertility with the annual removal of its nutrients in the meat of sheep and a few deer, until the only remedy is the leaf fall of a thousand, thousand birches. There will be doubters, but what they should not do is ignore the enthusiasm of the author. Change remains inevitable.

Ten years is a short time in the history of the world. Many aims of SNH are ones that those of us responsible for land would like to embrace, but timescales make it difficult for the rest of the world without going bust. Readers will have to form their own view of the usefulness of setting hypothetical figures to a perfectly valid dream. One thing, however, is certain. If Scotland cannot find its way to the heart of the dream, it can never become the land for which so many of us have fought.

Patrick Gordon-Duff-Pennington

L. GILL

We planted the trees today
In the sight of the sea,
And in the shadow of the sea gulls' wings.
It was an act of grace,
Not so graceful as the arc of the white birds' flight,
But an act of faith and defiance
None the less;
Some small atom of dust to fling
In the eyes of the world's destroyers
With their bombs
And their pledge to kill.
It will solve no problems
For a starving world,
Serve no material benefit;
But to those who come after it will show
That we had a belief which sustained us.
And so, today, we planted the trees
Underneath the wheeling wings,
With the breeze in our faces,
And in our minds
The thought of the shading leaves
Over the generations to come.

Patrick Gordon-Duff-Pennington

AUTHOR'S ACKNOWLEDGEMENTS

I am grateful to the committee, chaired by Dick Balharry, who steered me, and to the members of the Review Group, who encouraged, criticised and commented on the draft. However, many others, mostly those mentioned below, advised and assisted. Without their unstinting help, this book could not have been written. To those whom I may have forgotten to thank and acknowledge, I offer my apologies. Finally, I am, as always, indebted to my wife, Louise, for editorial help and constant support.

Stewart Ashworth, Scottish Agricultural College

Andrew Barton

Elizabeth Berry

Roger Burton, SNH

Robin Callander

Geordie Chalmer

Hugh Cheape

Douglas Clarke, Conservator, Grampian Conservancy, The Forestry Authority

Professor T Clutton-Brock, Cambridge University

Richard Cooke, Association of Deer Managers

Edwin Cross, SNH

Ivor Davies, Highland Birchwoods

Desmond Dugan, RSPB

Peter Duncan, SNH

Robert Dunsmore, Conservator, Highland Conservancy, The Forestry Authority

Dr John Fletcher

Lorne Gill, SNH

Nicola Fletcher

Ian A Fraser, School of Scottish Studies, Edinburgh University

Diana Gilbert, Highland Birchwoods

Patrick Gordon-Duff-Pennington, OBE, Chairman of the Deer Commission for Scotland

Alan Hampson, SNH

Dr Alison Hester, MLURI

Guy Holborne, Librarian, Lincoln's Inn, London

Sue Holt, SNH

John Kerr, SNH

Sir John Lister-Kaye, Bt

Jim McCarthy

Angus MacDonald, SNH

Simon McGowan, Blairgowrie Public Library

Colin Maclean, RDC

Catriona Marshall, SNH

M Matthew

Jill Matthews, SNH

David Minns, RSPB

Sally Moore

Dave Morris, The Ramblers' Association, Scotland

Michael Osborne, Royal Scottish Forestry Society

Dr D A Ratcliffe

Dr Peter Reynolds, SNH

Richard Sidgwick, West Highland Estates

Professor Brian Staines, Institute of Terrestrial Ecology

Grahame Steele, Aberdeen University Library

Fiona Stewart, MLURI

Lord Strathnaver

Dr Des Thompson, SNH

Ashleigh Tooth, SNH

Graham Tuley, formerly of the Forestry Authority

R Youngson, RDC

SUMMARY

Creag Meagaidh has been a National Nature Reserve (NNR) for ten years now, and this book describes the first decade of management. When it was acquired by the Nature Conservancy Council, now Scottish Natural Heritage, the land in the old forests of Aberarder and Moy had been grazed for centuries by deer, sheep, goats and cattle. These uses of the land had created a wet moorland in which trees were scarce, the situation prevailing in much of the Highlands. When the land was acquired by the NCC, the aim became to restore the ecological health of the land. This was to be achieved by reducing grazing pressure to enable native trees to grow tall, where previously they had been checked by browsing, and to enable the plant life of the corries to flourish. After ten years, the results are impressive, showing that a NNR can provide a unique opportunity for bold and

R. BALHARRY

Accelerated erosion and tracking – too many deer in the forest.

innovative management to benefit Scotland's natural heritage, with wider implications for land use. The book's purpose is to encourage owners and managers of other Highland estates to look at SNH's management to see if they could adapt some of it to their own land. It is the contention of the book that adoption of methods and policies tried at Creag Meagaidh would benefit the natural heritage and ecological health of the Highlands without necessarily incurring financial loss. Solutions tried at Creag Meagaidh are not a panacea, but do raise the possibility of other choices at a time when many 'traditional' uses of the land are under pressure.

This book traces the management of the land from an age when a largely kin-based society lived by subsistence farming and pastoralism; through the alternating fortunes of sheep-grazing and sport shooting from the mid-eighteenth to the mid-twentieth centuries; to the threat of monocultural afforestation in the mid-1980s that culminated in the purchase of the land and its declaration as a NNR. It describes in some detail the management that the NCC and SNH have pursued in order to restore an ecological balance.

Highland estates are usually managed for a variety of purposes, including agriculture, forestry and field sports. State support for these activities (except for field sports), in the form of grants and subsidies, is complex and varied, but influences decisions on all estates, even those heavily supported by an independent source of income. SNH wished to explore, as an alternative model, a system that could rebuild natural capital and, in the long run, use it sustainably; a different approach from that which had gone before, but one which is essential if the Highlands are to arrest their decline and fulfil their ecological potential.

CHAPTER 1: INTRODUCTION

P. & A. MACDONALD

In 1994, Sir William Gordon Cumming wrote that the grouse moor economy was finished, and that 'the decline is absolute and final...'. He recommended changes to land use in the Highlands that included conversion of much grouse moor to woodland, using native species. All hill sheep would be removed permanently and red deer and roe deer would be culled severely. A new kind of sporting estate would result – with new landscapes and new possibilities, 'a sporting paradise of a different kind'. The article, written in uncompromising terms, could have been considered provocative, yet there was not a word of disagreement in the correspondence columns of subsequent numbers of *Scottish Forestry*. A similar article in *The Field* by Sir John Lister-Kaye, and the extended version of his article, *Ill Fares the Land*, aroused only limited opposition, and that on points of detail rather than on the thrust of the writing. Changes of attitude to the management of hill land are detectable in the recent tendency of sale particulars for estates to go beyond the traditional form. In addition to describing the numbers of game taken each year, particulars may now include information about the estate being a place of great beauty and of scientific interest, and that part or all of it is a SSSI; this is seen as a bonus and not a disadvantage as in the past.

Intensely managed moorland may be appropriate in the eastern Highlands, but not in the west.

Changes in the hills over the past 50 years are forcing a reassessment of economic and ecological viability. Interaction of grazing pressure by sheep, whose numbers have increased four-fold over the past 50 years (Stevenson and Thompson, 1993), and the greatly increased herd of red deer together with the expansion of commercial forestry (Hester and Sydes, forthcoming; quoted in Stevenson and Thompson, 1993), and the loss of wintering grounds to hydro-schemes have aggravated land use problems in the Highlands to the point where change is essential. A drop in grouse numbers and loss of salmon in the rivers have brought things to a head.

In *Creag Meagaidh National Nature Reserve: an Historical Land Use Survey*, the late Roger O'Donovan wrote 'There have been many changes in ownership, management aims and ideals on estates large and small all over upper Badenoch' (O'Donovan, 1988). The same can be said for the Highlands as a whole. A study published in 1983 showed that only 12% of estates over 2000 hectares in the Highlands were under the same ownership in 1976 as in 1873. Sporting estates are likely to change hands more often than estates with a strong agricultural or forestry interest (Armstrong and Mather, 1983). New owners often have little to guide them on the management of their new acquisitions, other than in ways hallowed by the practices of the past two centuries. Unfortunately, the professional advisers to these new owners often have little experience in the management of land on sound ecological principles.

Many landowners wish to change but do not know how to do so without going bust.

The intention of this book is to show that, with the assurance of support from the Forestry Authority's (FA) Woodland Grant Scheme, and by making certain changes in the management of the deer, it should be possible for owners to move their estates towards environmental sustainability, while minimising financial risk. If these modifications are made, they should lead to gains in diversity (biological, landscape and land use) and biological productivity (such as an improvement in the condition of the deer). Landowners will increase the biological capital of the land in a real sense and not in the fictional way accepted by markets of the present day.

SNH's experience at Creag Meagaidh NNR in the old forests[1] of Aberarder and Moy has spanned only 10 years so far, so the project is still in its restoration phase, and data derived from it can give only provisional impressions. When restoration has been achieved, management will be able to move to a new sustainable phase. It is, however, clear that experience so far makes it timely to broadcast the Creag Meagaidh work more widely.

[1] Since the Middle Ages the word 'forest' has been used in Scotland to mean a hunting reserve, specifically for deer. This might or might not have trees in it (Gilbert, 1979).

CHAPTER II: BACKGROUND

The land use and management history of the estate, 1600–1985

Two former deer forests make up the area that is now the National Nature Reserve – the forests of Moy and part of Aberarder, which were part of the great feudal domain of the Gordon Lords of Huntly in 1600. They lie at the western extremity of Badenoch in the parish of Laggan, and Moy itself marches with Lochaber. For most of the outside world, the Highlands were still, at that time, *terra incognita*, separated from the rest of Scotland by their rugged terrain, difficult communications[1] and a different language, the Gaelic.[2]

For the people of Laggan, life was dominated through the seventeenth and the first half of the eighteenth century by the seasonal requirements of an agricultural way of life. Political disturbance brought its measure of misery, but famine and disease in the seventeenth century and famine and dispossession in the eighteenth century were the real scourges of the people (Whyte, 1979). Periods of crisis apart, life and agricultural practices continued much as they had done for generations, with the seasonal cycles of arable husbandry and pastoralism determining the people's activities. During the earlier part of this period, the men of Badenoch were listed along with their neighbours and kinsmen,

the MacDonells of Keppoch, the MacGregors in Rannoch and elsewhere, and many other clans, for their propensity for cattle raiding.[3] The Gaels raided far afield as this song from Rannoch suggests:

> *C'uime am biomaid gun eudail*
> Why should we be without cattle
> *Agus spréidh aig na Gallaibh?*
> and the Lowlanders have herds?
> *Gheibh sinn crodh as a'Mhaorainn*
> We will get cattle from the Mearns
> *Agus caorich a Gallaibh.*
> and sheep from Caithness.[4]

The standard settlement of the old Highlands was the *ferm toun* held under a joint tenancy by a group of people. The sites of four survive on the present NNR; at Aberarder, Innis nan Gall, Tullochcrom and Strath Chruineachdan. In addition, there were other communities at Comharsan, Rubha na Magach and Kyleross (Sinton, 1906). Each *ferm toun* was surrounded by its inbye arable land, its outbye land and, further away, by the community's grazing (unenclosed hill), for which the grazing rights were often held in common.[5,6]

Despite the Rising of 1715, the early eighteenth century was a time of increasing peace in the Highlands. The foremost chiefs were much involved in the cattle trade and were keen to exploit the natural resources of their lands, rather than lead the life of feuding warlords. The road-making achievements of General Wade between 1725 and 1737 (such as the road over the Corrieyairack Pass and the bridge at Garvamore),[7] and subsequently

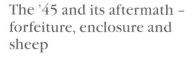

P. & A. MACDONALD

Corrieyairack Pass.

of his successor, Major Edward Caulfield, and the existence of the Independent Companies contributed to the settling of the Highlands. Many of the men of Badenoch found part-time employment in the Independent Companies, later to become the Black Watch. The government's withdrawal of the Black Watch from the Highlands for service in Flanders was one of the contributory factors that triggered the Jacobite Rising of 1745.

The '45 and its aftermath – forfeiture, enclosure and sheep

In August 1745, Cluny Macpherson, whose territory in Brae Badenoch included Aberarder, switched loyalties at the last moment and led his Independent Company out to join the Jacobite cause, instead of obeying the government's command to lead his men to join Lord Loudon's regiment of Highlanders. Cluny was an excellent commander and led his clan regiment ably throughout the campaign. The defeat of the Jacobites at Culloden (at which the Macphersons were not present) on 16 April 1746 left the Macphersons and their dependants desperately exposed to the vengeance of those whom they had humiliated: Cluny had to flee to France. His estates were forfeited and managed on behalf of the Crown by the Commissioners for the Forfeited Estates. The Commissioners' factor, Henry Butter, started the legal proceedings that enabled the eviction of the tenants in April 1770, when Aberarder was organised into a single holding (Sinton, 1906).[8]

In the eighteenth century, the better-off who left the Highlands often emigrated to North America (Bumsted, 1982; Hunter, 1994). The second half of the eighteenth century was a period of rapid population growth throughout Europe (Richards, 1982). In the Highlands of Scotland this increase in human numbers, coupled with clearance, emigration and occasional famine, added to the upheaval of the times as the old clan society completed its government-sponsored disintegration.

The entry for Laggan in the first Statistical Account of 1790 records 20,000 sheep in the parish, the result of more than 20 years of accelerated agricultural change, promoted by the Commissioners for the Forfeited Estates. It also recorded that one of the two main landowners in the parish was Colonel Macpherson, son of the hero of the '45, and restored to his family's estates in 1784 (Macpherson, 1893). The parish minister of Laggan in 1790 was James Grant, whose wife Anne Grant's book,

Letters from the Mountains, gives a sympathetic account of the life of the district at that time. After he died in 1801, Mrs Grant continued to manage her husband's farm and left valuable accounts of the farming practices of the time, including transhumance,[9] shortly to become a thing of the past throughout most of the Highlands.[10]

In December 1792, Mrs Grant commented in a letter to a friend on the rush into sheep and the disturbances that this had caused that year in Sutherland '....The only cause of complaint in Scotland is the rage for sheep farming. The families removed on that account are often as numerous as our own. The poor people have neither language, money nor education to push their way anywhere else; though they often possess feelings and principles that might almost rescue human nature from the reproach which false philosophy and false refinement have brought upon it.' (Grant, 1845).[11]

By 1840, the New Statistical Account recorded the presence of 40,000 sheep in the parish of Laggan, and even more changes were on their way.

The coming of the Ramsdens

In 1844, Old Cluny – grandson of Ewan of the '45 – let the estate of Ardverikie on the south side of Loch Laggan to the Marquess of Abercorn. Lord Abercorn had already had eight years' experience of managing Ben Alder as a deer forest. He removed the sheep from Ardverikie and released a number of hinds that he had obtained mainly from Glenfiddich. In 1850, Lord Henry Bentinck took over the lease, followed in 1869 by Sir John Ramsden (O'Donovan, 1988).

Sir John erected 45 miles of deer fence, 35 miles of sheep fence and built 40 miles of roads. For 15 years he planted one million trees a year (P Gordon-Duff-Pennington, personal communication). A condition of the lease from Cluny included a clause arranging for compensation for improvements at waygoing. Such was the scale of the Ramsdens' expenditure that the Macphersons could not afford to pay the compensation when Cluny died, and the estate passed to Sir John (O'Donovan, 1988).

Sir John Ramsden bought the surrounding estates of Ben Alder, Dalwhinnie, Inverpattack, Strathmashie, Glenshero and, in 1877, Moy and Braeroy. In 1929, Aberarder was joined to this great complex of deer forests, sheep farms, fishings, grouse moors and woodland operations, when the Macphersons sold up (O'Donovan, 1988).

Visitors and climbers

At about the same time that sport began to take over much of the Highlands, others with different interests became active. Charles Darwin visited Glen Roy in 1838 to inspect the 'Parallel Roads', and in 1840 the great Swiss glaciologist Louis Agassiz[12] visited the glen while on a visit to Scotland to attend the annual meeting of the British Association for the Advancement of Science, which was held in Glasgow that year.[13] At much the same time came the

BY KIND PERMISSION OF
HM THE QUEEN

Watercolour by Queen Victoria of Creag Meagaidh, painted during her visit to Ardverikie in 1847.

walkers and then, when the first generation of alpinists had handed on their skills to another generation, out came the climbers looking for new places on which to try their skills.[14] Early attempts showed that prospects for rock climbing were not particularly good because of vegetation on the cliffs, although they would make excellent ice climbing in winter. So it has proved increasingly since the 1930s when the cliffs of Coire Ardair first submitted to winter ascents.

Hydro-electricity

In 1934, the effects of another of the great attempts to develop the Highlands began to impact on the surrounding landscape. In that year the British Aluminium Company's hydro-electric dam on the River Spean at Rough Burn was completed. Resultant flooding of low ground around the loch, and later planting and fencing along the southern slopes of Glen Spean and elsewhere, greatly reduced winter grazing available to stags from the central and western parts of the Monadhliath.[15]

The Hill Farming Act, 1946

The next great change in terms of land use history at Aberarder was the passing in 1946 of the Hill Farming Act. This, and subsequent legislation, ensured subsidies that underpinned the hill farming industry until the accession of the United Kingdom to the European Economic Community

(now the European Union), when the provisions of the Common Agricultural Policy took over support of the agricultural industry.

Captain Neil Usher acquired the lease of Aberarder at Martinmas 1947 and farmed there until 1957. Sheep and a few cattle were back on the hill and, in the spirit of the time, considerable works of agricultural improvement were undertaken. In 1957, Captain Usher left and the sheep stocks were taken over by the Ramsden estate. By the time that Loch Laggan Estates sold Moy and Aberarder to Fountain Forestry in 1983, stalking had replaced sheep as the main activity of the estates. The last significant sheep flock left the present NNR in 1977 (O'Donovan, 1988).

Socioeconomic factors, farming, forestry and game management

The summary of the history of land use in the forests of Moy and Aberarder has given some indication of the way that sheep farming and sporting estate management have interacted over the last century and a half. The Ramsdens had been heavily involved in forestry from the 1850s. Sir John's forestry was of a pioneering kind in its use of exotic coniferous species (O'Donovan, 1988), and a foreshadowing of things to come. However, included among the exotics were considerable numbers of Scots Pine of native origin (Graham Tuley, personal communication), and the relevance of this will become apparent later. Sheep farming, field sports and forestry were introduced with the intention of providing the owners of the land with income in a cash economy. Their inspiration was the drive that followed the '45 to pacify the Highlands and make them economically productive, a part of the process of agricultural change led by the agricultural improvers of the eighteenth century. Sheep farming, that great hope of the second half of the eighteenth century, has struggled on,

through trade cycles from relative cheer to depression, and now survives, heavily subsidised, as a way of keeping people in the countryside. Forestry can only be undertaken with considerable subsidy (a warning to other nations who strip their forest and do not understand the huge cost of restoration). Survey after survey shows that sporting estates are not economically viable. Their capital values stem from a perception of them that has more to do with Thorstein Veblen's understanding of conspicuous consumption, as described in his *Theory of the Leisure Class*, than in any understanding of sustainability and land use (Jarvie, 1980; McGilvray and Perman, 1991).

Land use and forestry from 1945 to 1988

The end of the second world war saw renewed interest in the question of Highland land use. Much land was judged to have lost fertility as a result of excessive grazing (Darling, 1955). Cattle were seen as a way of restoring fertility to the hill, and forestry as part of a range of land uses that would help to ease the balance of payments deficit. It would bring

L. GILL

Grazing cattle can be as important for conservation as for the management of hill farming.

employment to the Highlands and contribute to the restoration of fertility to land that was to be described as wet desert (Darling, 1969). Private owners were offered the Dedication Scheme whereby ground, dedicated to timber production by a management plan approved by the Forestry Commission, would receive exemptions from taxation. This was a constructive way of reviving the forest industry, ravaged by two world wars. It would restore a strategic reserve of timber and, in due course, reduce the country's dependence on imports. It was not long before a sharp-eyed accountant called Rankin realised the implications for his clients, who paid up to 98% tax on their income. Thus was born the tax-efficient forest industry (Tomkins, 1986). Until 1988, when the Finance Act ended tax-driven forestry by taking it out of the taxation system, great areas of the Highlands were covered with drab (but often high yield class) plantations, mainly of Sitka spruce. The industry could never have covered so much ground had it not been for the discovery of techniques for planting peat land that had previously been unplantable. As ground available for commercial afforestation ran

P. & A. MACDONALD

A look across the land that would have become a plantation. Aberarder farmhouse lies ahead.

out or became too expensive, the eyes of the foresters turned to the peat lands of the North.[16] They were stopped by hostile public opinion after a campaign ably fought by conservationists.

Changes in forest policy

They were halted in Caithness, but also at Aberarder and Moy, for what was to become the Creag Meagaidh NNR was one of the signal battles in this campaign. It led on the one hand to the end of tax-driven forestry through the Finance Act of 1988, but also confirmed the need for local authorities to draw up Indicative Forestry Strategies. It was also a contributory factor in the reorganisation of the NCC and its reconstitution in Scotland together with the Countryside Commission for Scotland, as Scottish Natural Heritage (SNH). There is another angle, however. In 1957, the Zuckerman Report established that any future world war was likely to be thermonuclear, and thus short.[17] The idea of a strategic supply of timber for a long war was no longer tenable, and the motivation for the forestry industry changed to import substitution and the provision of employment in the countryside (Callander, 1995). By the late 1960s, increased demand for access and interest in landscaping the badly designed blocks of timber that had been planted since the 1930s and 1940s led to the commissioning of a report by the distinguished landscape architect, Dame Sylvia Crowe. The outcome was confirmation of the need for a shift of emphasis to take account of these interests. Recognition in several reports of the poor economic return to the community (*Forestry in Great Britain – An Inter-departmental Cost/Benefit Analysis,* HMSO, 1972 and *Review of Forestry Commission's Objectives and Achievements,* National Audit Office, 1986, quoted in Callander, 1995) from the forest industry and pressure from environmentalists tilted the scales through the 1980s. The first Woodland Grant Scheme (WGS1), introduced in October 1988, insisted, for the first time, on the inclusion of a proportion of broadleaves in coniferous plantations.[18] Since WGS1, Woodland Grant Schemes have broadened the scope of aid to encourage a wide range of objectives and consider in detail the impact of proposals on

L.GILL

Young plantation in Glen Spean.

landscape, nature conservation, public access, water and archaeology (R Dunsmore, personal communication). All this has tilted the balance away from the production forestry of a generation ago. The story of Creag Meagaidh fits into the middle of this history of changing policy and attitudes towards the growing of trees.

Acquisition of the estate by the NCC and declaration of the NNR

The first citation of a Site of Special Scientific Interest in 1964 in the area of what is now the Creag Meagaidh NNR was for the geological interest of the ground between Rubha na Magach and Am Meall.[19] That of 1975 for a much larger SSSI (6986 hectares) followed the survey work of D A Ratcliffe between 1956 and 1959. Dr Ratcliffe's report recognised the unbroken succession of natural and semi-natural vegetation types that run from the shores of Loch Laggan to the summit of Creag Meagaidh at 1128 metres and described the important montane heaths on the summit plateau. The area of *Racomitrium* (woolly-fringe

P. & A. MACDONALD

Loch shore to summit plateau – Aberarder to the Uinneag.

moss) heath at levels over 900 metres is one of the largest in the Highlands and is the preferred breeding habitat for dotterel. At present, the site includes the largest area of semi-natural woodlands in the upper Spean catchment area. Its description in 1975 included the following statement: 'This mountain of Moine schist reaches 3700 feet and contains a magnificent corrie with 1000-foot cliffs. There are many interesting montane plants, mainly on non-calcareous rocks and an extensive development of *Racomitrium* heath on the eastern ridges. Exposures of pegmatite veins cutting Moine schists also occur'. These factors justified notification of the area as a SSSI and its subsequent establishment as a National Nature Reserve, according to criteria set out in the *Nature Conservation Review* that had been undertaken in the 1970s. Dr Ratcliffe, then the NCC's Chief Scientist, undertook a review of British habitats and the selection of national nature reserves (Moore, 1987). This attempted, for the first time, to put all SSSIs in the British Isles into one conceptual framework. Certain criteria were chosen on which to assess sites and their importance for nature conservation. These were size, diversity, naturalness, rarity, fragility, typicalness, recorded history, position in an ecological/geographical unit, potential value and intrinsic appeal. All SSSIs were subjected to review in the light of these criteria and the results were published in the two-volume *A Nature Conservation Review* (Ratcliffe, 1977).

The sale of Moy and part of Aberarder

In 1979, a combination of circumstances brought financial difficulty to Loch Laggan Estates, the owners of the forests of Aberarder and Moy. The new Conservative government led by Mrs Thatcher told the Forestry Commission to cut their deficit. On the international scene, there was a glut of Canadian timber. The price of saw logs dropped from £23/tonne to £6/tonne. Depending for income on sales of timber, Loch Laggan Estates found themselves with a cash flow crisis. The problem could be resolved only by laying off eight men in their forestry squad, or selling land (P Gordon-Duff-Pennington, personal communication). The decision was to sell Moy and that part of Aberarder that lay to the west of Coire nan Gall and followed a line down the Piper's Burn to the east of the steading at Aberarder. The land was sold in 1983, the year in which the Creag Meagaidh SSSI was renotified under the Wildlife and Countryside Act of 1981. It was bought by Fountain Forestry,[20] who proposed to plant a large area of the SSSI with Sitka spruce. There was public dismay and a campaign was mounted to prevent it happening. There followed negotiations between Fountain Forestry and the NCC to safeguard the site through a voluntary management agreement. Objections to the use of the site for commercial forestry hinged on the loss of vegetational types that this would cause at middle range between Loch Laggan and the summit plateau; the loss of important winter feeding grounds to eagles; and the loss of habitat (including nesting areas) to birds such as dunlin, golden plover, hen harriers and short-eared owls.[21] The extent of commercial forestry throughout Glen Spean[22] was such that the slopes leading to Creag Meagaidh from Loch Laggan were the last in the area with a complete altitudinal succession of natural or semi-natural vegetation. As far as walkers and climbers were concerned, the proposal for a big plantation across the lower ground threatened a restriction of

access to the tops and so had to be fought. There followed a fierce campaign, led by environmentalists, climbers and walkers.[23] David Bellamy threatened to lie in front of the bulldozers if the plan was allowed. David Minns of RSPB and Dave Morris, now of the Ramblers' Association (but then of the NCC in Aviemore), were among the most active and effective campaigners. The application was discussed at a meeting of the Regional Advisory Committee of the Forestry Commission's Highland Conservancy and was referred to the Secretary of State,

L. CAMPBELL

Dead deer provide food for eagles.

George Younger, who told Fountain Forestry that they might plant half the ground they had wanted to afforest. At that, Fountain Forestry abandoned the project, refused to enter a management agreement with the NCC to safeguard the SSSI and agreed to sell the ground.

In March 1985, the purchase of Moy Estate from Fountain Forestry was concluded and the NCC assumed ownership of the 3940 hectares of the SSSI, including the main massif and ridge system of Creag Meagaidh. At that time the Council felt that its portfolio of mountain properties was sufficient and it preferred to have management agreements with private proprietors rather than incur the expenses of ownership (J McCarthy, personal communication). Fountain Forestry had bought the land for £300,000 in 1983 and sold what was to become the NNR to the NCC in 1985 for £431,000. The increase of £131,000 in the price of the land in so short a time resulted from the value added to the ground by virtue of it having planting permission for 530 hectares. This amounted to compensation for not destroying part of a SSSI. The need to pay for the development value of the ground was enshrined in the Wildlife and Countryside Act of 1981 and has been the subject of much criticism by conservationists. A developer who wished to alter a listed building would not be compensated for not altering it. Conservationists throughout the country asked why anybody should be compensated for not being allowed to spoil a SSSI. The landowners' point of view was that compensation should be paid for an asset that was being sterilised for reasonable development. Whatever the case then, it is no longer possible for forestry applicants to achieve the same compensation as before for not destroying a SSSI. The value of any forestry grants forgone may not be taken into account when assessing compensation payable, if SNH alone objects to a planting proposal (R Burton, personal communication).

The land owned by the NCC was officially declared the Creag Meagaidh NNR by the late Sir Robert Cowan, then chairman of the Highlands and Islands Development Board, at a ceremony at Aberarder Farm in May 1986. Thus was marked the arrival of another use of land in the area.

In a letter to *The Scotsman* of 25 March 1985, Roger Smith of the Scottish Wild Land Group wrote, 'Let us leave the NCC to manage Creag Meagaidh as a nature reserve and show thereby that conservation can be a positive use of our magnificent wild land.'

[1] In the 1590s, however, the map maker Timothy Pont travelled through the region. The findings of his travels were included in Blaeu's map of 1654, and this gives the first cartographical information about Laggan (Macfarlane, 1908). The map does not mention Moy, the western part of the present National Nature Reserve, but identifies Kylleross (Coille Rais), Aberarder, Tullochcrom and Lagan Coinnich, all place names used today.

[2] Outside the Highlands, Gaelic was probably spoken in Fife until about 1350 and hung on in Galloway until the sixteenth century (H Cheape, personal communication).

[3] The clans that were most inclined to raid were those whose territory contained least inbye land and who did not hold their land by right of charter, i.e. as the MacDonells of Keppoch, they were tenants at will of another clan.

[4] This magnificent song ('Bothan Airigh am Braigh Raithneach') is printed in W J Watson's *Bardachd Gaidhlig* and is on a cassette sung by Catherine Anne Macphee, who learned it from the late Revd William Matheson.

[5] On the subject of place names as indicators of settlement, Professor Barrow has said that 'The overwhelming majority of habitation names in the rural areas of Scotland, either still in use or at least surviving on the modern map, had already come into existence before about 1250' (Barrow, 1981).

[6] The lands of Aberarder belonged to the Bishopric of Moray until the Reformation (1560), when they passed to the Grants of Freuchie. In 1696, the Grants feued the lands to Alexander Macdonald, in Achnacoichen of Brae Lochaber, an offshoot of the Macdonells of Keppoch. Representatives of Alexander Macdonald sold three of his four ploughgates to the family of Mackintosh. In 1726, Lachlan Mackintosh of Mackintosh agreed to dispose of these ploughgates, in the form of wadset, to Macpherson of Cluny. The old wadsetters and possessors do not seem to have been disturbed so the Macdonalds remained at Aberarder (Fraser-Mackintosh, 1897).

[7] The Kingshouse nearby probably dates from 1740.

[8] The Reverend Robert Macpherson, a half-pay army chaplain, acquired the farm and cleared about 80 families to make way for sheep farming (Fraser-Mackintosh, 1897, 1890). In 1780, the family of Sinton from Teviotdale occupied Aberarder.

[9] The seasonal movement of livestock to take account of the availability of grazing.

[10] Green patches on the hillsides often indicate the sites of abandoned shielings and in many places the foundations of the huts that the people occupied during the summer months may be made out, as at the shieling site by the Coille Coire Chrannaig.

[11] Commenting on agricultural improvements carried out at that time, and seen from a different point of view, Dr Thomas Sinton, the descendant of the Border farmers who had taken a lease of Aberarder in 1780, wrote 'It is to be feared, however, that in almost every case the enterprising men who carried out these improvements met with disappointment and loss – usually financial ruin.' (Sinton, 1910).

[12] Agassiz was an opponent of Darwin and later became professor of Zoology at Harvard University.

[13] He was the first to identify the parallel roads for what they were – the shore lines of former ice-dammed lakes.

[14] The great cliffs of Coire Ardair proved a compelling draw, but the first serious exploration did not take place until April 1896 when Harold Raeburn and Messrs Tough and Brown climbed Pinnacle Buttress via Easy Gully (*SMC Journal,* Vol. 4, no. 2, September 1896).

[15] These areas had attracted stags from Braeroy and Glenshero, and possibly from Aberchalder, Glendoe and Cullachy in the past (O'Donovan, 1988).

[16] There is an analogy here with the ending of the Hydro Board's expansion in the 1960s. All the suitable sites had been dammed and plans to dam Rannoch Moor were too expensive for the Treasury. By that time, too, conservationists had become strong enough to sway public opinion.

[17] Since 1989 and the ending of the Cold War, this is questionable.

[18] The Broadleaved Woodland Scheme had been introduced in 1985.

[19] It was described as a 'striking exposure of pegmatite veins of quartzo-feldspathic material in Moine schists' (NCC Management Plan, 1987).

[20] In August, the Forestry Commission notified the NCC of an application by Moy estate (through Fountain Forestry) to plant 1113.7 acres (530 ha) on the slopes of Creag Meagaidh itself.

[21] All Annex 1 species under the European Birds' Directive and so worthy of special protection.

[22] Eighty per cent of the glen had been afforested by the time that Fountain Forestry put in its application to plant at Moy and Aberarder.

[23] Among whom were the following: the RSPB, the Mountaineering Council of Scotland, the Badenoch and Strathspey Conservation Group, the Scottish Countryside Activities' Council, the North-East Mountaineering Trust, the Scottish Wild Land Group and the Scottish Wildlife Trust.

CHAPTER III: TEN YEARS OF MANAGEMENT CHANGE 1986–1996

Introduction

The last chapter gave an account of the historical background of the forests of Moy and Aberarder. Now, we should consider the setting that has enabled the NCC and SNH to manage the estate differently from its previous owners, who ran it as a sheep farm and deer forest, or from the owners who might have managed it for plantation forestry.

The name of the reserve

The new National Nature Reserve (NNR) was formed from parts of the forests of Moy and Aberarder. These names had, for centuries, clear meanings for the Gaelic-speaking people of the area. The mountain at the back of the forests was a part of this landscape, but does not seem to have enjoyed its present fame.[1] For the Gaels of Laggan it seems that the hill was a backdrop, but not a topographical icon. The naming of the reserve after the mountain reveals a difference of perspective. The mountaineers, who had found that the cliffs of Coire Ardair were excellent for ice-

P. & A. MACDONALD

The cliffs at Coire Ardair, with the Lochan a' Choire below.

climbing, focused on them. Others more concerned with landscape looked to the summit as a great centrepiece from which views could be seen; the naturalists had recognised the ecological interest of the place. As a focus for the campaign against commercial afforestation and for its acquisition as a NNR, Creag Meagaidh became a beacon.

The nineteenth century deer forest and its legacy to the natural heritage

Red deer, their management and interactions with other forms of land use, have been controversial down the centuries.[2] The creation of the deer forests of the last century stirred up bitter feelings in the Highlands and beyond, because of the evictions of tenants that resulted from their establishment in a number of cases, but more often as a result of their aggravation of the crofters' land hunger, particularly from the 1860s onwards (Richards 1982; Watson and Allan, 1990). There were also conflicts with sheep farming.

Much was written from the point of view of the sportsman; including William Scrope's *Art of Deer Stalking* (1838), the Marchioness of Breadalbane's *High Tops of the Black Mount* (1907) and Allan Gordon Cameron's *The Wild Red Deer of Scotland* (1923). A great deal was written, also, attacking the new sporting estates, mainly from the point

of view of the dispossessed (Marx, 1976; MacKenzie, 1883); there were also government reports and inquiries (such as the Napier Report of 1884 and the Royal Commission – Highlands and Islands – of 1892). Henry Evans, father-in-law of Allan Cameron, was a prototype in his enlightened attitude to deer and their management in Jura in the late 1800s. However, nothing was published about red deer and their ecology that had any basis in science until Frank Fraser Darling's *A Herd of Red Deer* (1937). The influence of this work became important, after the establishment of the Nature Conservancy in 1949, in helping to define a need to acquire an area of country in which red deer could be studied. It was hoped that the findings of research would increase knowledge of their biology and that this would be generally applicable to the management of the species in the Scottish Highlands.

In 1970, the small deer forest of Inshriach on the north-west side of the Cairngorms came on the market and was bought by the NCC, so adding to Invereshie, which had been acquired in 1954. It was apparent that the native pine forest for which the reserve had been acquired was not regenerating because of heavy grazing by red deer, both resident and from the neighbouring estates of Rothiemurchus to the north and Glenfeshie to the south. A decision by Rothiemurchus to remove many hinds in order to start a deer farm resulted in a reduction of grazing pressure and the creation of a buffer zone between populations of hinds. In 1974/75, the NCC decided to manage the deer in the Inshriach National Nature Reserve with the important objective of ensuring the survival of the pine woodland by natural regeneration, rather than manage it as a sporting estate. The red deer at Invereshie and Inshriach were heavily culled. Evidence from Rum, where the NCC had been studying red deer since the island's acquisition as a nature reserve in 1957, was beginning to suggest that anxiety about a 'vacuum effect'[3] was likely to prove ill-founded. In Rum, however, the NCC had no neighbours, unlike in Badenoch and Strathspey. At Inshriach, the neighbouring landowner (the late Lord Dulverton) was anxious that deer might move out of Glenfeshie into Inshriach after a heavy cull. In the event, this did not happen to any significant extent. Nevertheless, neighbours elsewhere expressed similarly understandable anxieties: diplomacy would have to become as important a skill as the practice of conservation science. The insights gained from the management of red deer at Inshriach were later applied at Creag Meagaidh.

L. CAMPBELL

Red deer stag in Caledonian pine forest.

The management plan of 1987

The management plan for Creag Meagaidh of 1987 lists the aims and objectives of management of the reserve. These were:

1. To allow ecosystems to evolve with minimum interference.

2. To encourage regeneration and extension of native forests and boreal scrub vegetation.

3. To fulfil legal obligations.

4. To consult neighbours over management policies.

5. To encourage appreciation and study of the reserve.

6. To encourage outdoor recreational activities that depend on the natural qualities and character of the reserve.

The writer of the plan observes that, although no irreversible damage seemed to have been done, 'At present, grazing impact is nearly maximal. No tree regeneration is taking place except in inaccessible places such as cliff faces or in highly disturbed areas such as road sides. Primarily the deer population is responsible for this although sheep from neighbouring estates may also cause significant damage. If left unchecked, mature trees acting as seed sources will eventually die and the potential for rejuvenating the woodland will be lost.' (Creag Meagaidh Management Plan, 1987). This is the start line. The forests of Aberarder and Moy had been bought in 1985. Some culling of deer had been done and the exclusion of sheep attempted, but a huge task lay ahead.

The reserve's boundaries – march dykes and fences

The visitor to Creag Meagaidh NNR usually arrives by car and parks in the reserve's car park below Aberarder Farm. Let us start from here on an imaginary circuit. We should walk down to the A86 and then west towards Moy at the western boundary of the NNR. The shore of Loch Laggan is the southern boundary. At Moy, we should strike north and walk along the wall of Moy that marks the ancient boundary between Badenoch and Lochaber. The age of the dyke is uncertain, but it may well have been built in the late eighteenth century as part of the improvements carried out by tenants after 1770. Starting at the roadside of the A86, it crosses the shoulder of Creag Mhor and then dips west towards Lochan na Cailliche. There is a gap in the dyke of about 750 metres, where its line crosses a moss of deep peat and is replaced by a fence. North of the moss, the dyke rises to Creag na Cailliche. From there, it follows the crest of the ridge, high up on the shoulder

Creag Meagaidh
National Nature Reserve

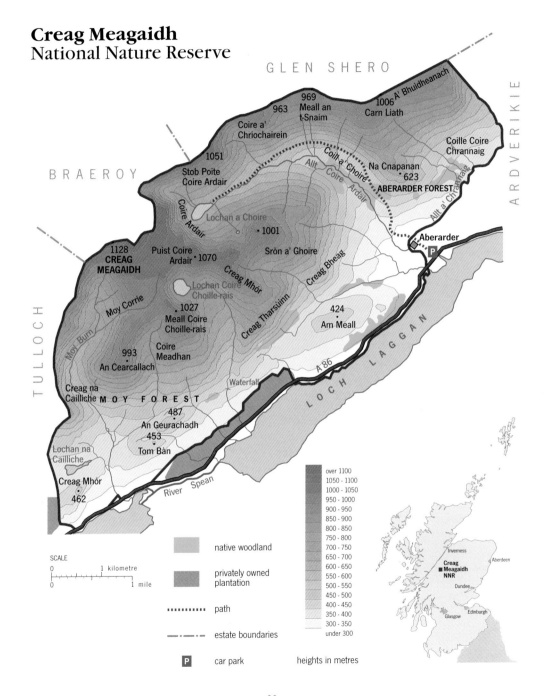

GLEN SHERO

BRAEROY

TULLOCH

ARDVERIKIE

A' Bhuidheanach

969
Meall an
t-Snaim

963

1006
Carn Liath

Coire a'
Chriochairein

Coille Coire
Chrannaig

1051
Stob Poite
Coire Ardair

Coill a' Choire

Na Cnapanan
• 623
ABERARDER FOREST

Allt Coire Ardair

Allt a' Chrannaig

Coire Ardair

Lochan a Choire

• 1001

Aberarder

1128
CREAG
MEAGAIDH

Puist Coire
Ardair • 1070

Sròn a' Ghoire

Creag Bheag

Lochan Coire
Choille-rais

Creag Mhór

Moy Corrie

• 1027
Meall Coire
Choille-rais

Creag Tharsúinn

424
•
Am Meall

LAGGAN

Moy Burn

Coire
Meadhan

993
•
An Cearcallach

A 86

Creag na
Cailliche MOY FOREST

Waterfall

LOCH

487
•
An Geurachadh

453
•
Tom Bàn

Lochan na
Cailliche

Creag Mhór
•
462

River Spean

SCALE

0   1 kilometre

0   1 mile

native woodland

privately owned
plantation

•••••••••• path

—•—•—•— estate boundaries

P   car park

over 1100
1050 - 1100
1000 - 1050
950 - 1000
900 - 950
850 - 900
800 - 850
750 - 800
700 - 750
650 - 700
600 - 650
550 - 600
500 - 550
450 - 500
400 - 450
350 - 400
300 - 350
under 300

heights in metres

Inverness

Aberdeen

Creag
Meagaidh
NNR

Dundee

Glasgow

Edinburgh

P. & A. MACDONALD

The Dyke of Moy.

of Creag Meagaidh. In 1985, this wall was in a state of disrepair. It was clear, however, that if restored it would be useful for controlling deer and sheep. The well-known firm of R J McLeod, civil engineers for the upgrading of a section of the A86 at the western end of the reserve, approached SNH for ideas for a sponsored project and the Moy wall was suggested. R J McLeod then made a generous contribution and Tulloch Estate helped with funds, providing access for the work to be carried out. With this assistance and money from SNH, the dyke was restored in 1994.

Continuing our imaginary beating of the bounds, we should climb the rising shoulder of the hill towards the summit and then follow the ridge round, dipping down by the Uinneag Coire Ardair before continuing along the plateau to Carn Liath (1006 m) and A'Bhuidheanach before descending by Coire nan Gall to pick up the line of the deer fence that runs from there down to Aberarder, marking the march with Aberarder East, a part of Ardverikie Estate. This shield fence, erected in 1985, had a double purpose: preventing deer and sheep wandering in from the east and helping to funnel deer on the nature reserve into the live catching paddock.

Fencing at Creag Meagaidh – the debate and the decisions

Fencing has been an important subject at Creag Meagaidh because the presence or lack of it has been central to the management of the deer and the natural regeneration of woodland. Until recently, it had been thought that landowners wishing their forestry to survive had to fence out the deer. On a limited scale and particularly in landscapes of enclosure, this is reasonable; but, in open and supposedly wild landscapes, the fence is a visual blight and ecologically suspect. The arguments for and against deer fencing are often rehearsed. The main argument in favour is that fencing achieves something definite by exclusion or enclosure, and that it is immediately effective. Moreover, it gives a yardstick beside which regeneration in open country can be measured. The counter arguments are that it is extremely expensive to erect and maintain. If it is breached in a time of deep snow and deer get into an exclosure, it can be difficult to expel them. Their exclusion from a block of land intensifies grazing pressure elsewhere, if it is not linked to reductions in population density and may reduce wintering ground formerly open to them. Fencing can block traditional routes and face deer with death, particularly when weakened by starvation in late winter,

or their displacement may cause problems on other land. The exclusion of deer also removes the beneficial effects of clearings made by them and the reduction of competition from other vegetation (SNH Policy Paper *Red Deer and the Natural Heritage*, 1994). It is increasingly accepted that the arguments against relying on fencing on the open hill are stronger than those in favour. Long-term costs of extensive woodland regeneration where fencing is used also have to be considered. These include the impacts of fencing on black grouse and capercaillie. Work done by the RSPB and the Game Conservancy has shown that both deer fences and ordinary stock fences are responsible for the death of black grouse and capercaillie. At Abernethy, where the RSPB removed fences in 1991 and 1992, black grouse numbers have tripled in the last five years (D Dugan, personal communication) and capercaillie have begun to recover (S Taylor, personal communication).[4] As regards landscape and access, fences are visually intrusive and restrictive. They tend to create even-aged stands of trees. When the fences eventually come down and the grazing pressure is still high, all that is achieved is more trees with the field layer becoming overgrazed again (P Duncan, personal communication). In practice, it is important to learn to minimise the use of fences as numbers of deer drop, not least from the point of view of cost.

For the reasons just outlined, it was decided at the beginning of the NCC's tenure of Creag Meagaidh to cull deer to a level that would allow natural regeneration of the woodland. Fencing would be relied on as little as possible.

H. MACKAY

Volunteers from Aberdeen take down the fence at Am Meall.

There was, however, uncertainty about the patterns of movement of deer and sheep, and fears were expressed that heavy culling might not result in the desired effect of reduction without invasion from neighbouring estates (the so-called 'vacuum effect' – see also the comments of Richard Sidgwick later in this chapter). In anticipation of such a possibility, the deer fence north of Am Meall was erected. It followed a line running from an enclosure belonging to Fountain Forestry at Moy along to Aberarder, making an exclosure of 350 hectares to protect any regeneration of woodland within that area. As we have read, a shield fence was built in 1986 from a point east of Aberarder farmhouse up into the Coire nan Gall.

The fence at Am Meall cost £10,000 and was a success, ensuring the survival of the regenerating woodland. At a moment when faith in the absence of a 'vacuum effect' was uncertain, some insurance was in place against heavy browsing damage. There was also a control against which progress outside the exclosure could be compared. In 1995, following the successful reduction in deer numbers, the fence was removed with all the benefits described earlier. There was, in addition, the added advantage of removing an obstacle to walkers and cross-country skiers (R Balharry, personal communication).

Habitat management and regeneration

'The area of moss/sedge heath is one of the largest in the Highlands. There are, besides, large areas of snowbed vegetation and extensive areas of ungrazed ledge vegetation on the massive cliff systems of Coire Ardair.' (SNH Management Plan, 1995)

Existing habitats

The range of habitats represented at Creag Meagaidh may be divided into the relatively stable montane environment above 800 metres, where human impacts have been least, and the dynamic habitats below the tree line, where the impacts of past land use have been greatest. On the summit plateau above the tree line, the montane heath represents the climax vegetation for that environment. The removal of sheep and reduction of the deer will stabilise further the

Racomitrium/Carex (moss/sedge) heath and begin to reverse a recent tendency for it to turn to grassland, which has occurred as a result of enrichment of the soil by animal dung and damage to the moss by trampling and grazing (Halcrow, 1994). The montane willow scrub will also benefit from fewer grazing mouths, but the changes will be relatively slow in comparison with what has already happened below 800 m in the last ten years.

L.GILL

The summit plateau – snowbed vegetation.

D. GOWANS

Looking down to Loch Laggan from the slopes of Na Cnaponan.

deer and sheep. Since then, smaller numbers of deer and sheep have allowed the vegetational succession to proceed from communities dominated by grasses to ones dominated by herbs and shrubs.

The woodlands: a history of decline

The management plan of 1987 described the regeneration of existing birchwood as one of its aims and stated that the extension of the woodland was to be encouraged. Owing to the intensity of grazing, there was very little sign of any regeneration from the remaining birchwoods. It was feared that the age of the surviving trees, with the possible lack of viable seed, might mean that the birch woodland on the slopes of Creag Meagaidh had a limited prospect of survival.

Below 800 metres, there is a mosaic of habitats: grassland, heath and flush plant communities with extensive birchwoods that make up one of the largest areas of native woodland in the upper Spey area. Until 1986, these plant communities were suppressed by

Five thousand years ago,[5] the Highlands and much of the rest of Scotland up to the tree line were covered with woodland,[6] perhaps as much as 65% (McVean and Ratcliffe, 1962; Usher and Thompson, 1988). In the west Highlands, oak forest had succeeded the pine that had been there in an earlier post-glacial phase (Bennett in Aldhous, 1995). In the drier and more continental east, pine forests still predominated. The introduction of agriculture and pastoral ways of life around 4500 years ago led to forest clearance and, as the number of people and their stock increased and climatic changes occurred, the landscape became ever barer. The clearing of the woods was not always one way, because runs of famines and catastrophic events, such as epidemic disease in the Middle Ages, would reduce the human population for a little and give time for the forest to recover for a while. The trend, however, was down, although the rate and extent of deforestation varied from one area to another. In Sutherland, for example, the first extensive clearance of forest was probably about 3700 years ago, whereas in the west Grampian area the first extensive clearances may not have been happening until around 400 years ago (H J B Birks in Usher and Thompson, 1988). The perception that deforestation was a consequence of eighteenth century sheep farming may be correct for much of the country, only to the extent that new waves of sheep continued to prevent forest regeneration, as did the expansion of the deer forests after 1860. Although fire was probably used for some form of woodland management from Mesolithic times, possibly to encourage the growth of hazel, alder and willow, or for hunting purposes, it was not until Bronze Age times (about 4000 BP) that it was used to develop and maintain an open landscape (Edwards in Smout, 1993).[7] By the fifteenth century, legislation was being

enacted to protect woodland from the effects of muir burn (Tait, 1928). Despite the development of an increasingly open landscape, however, relict woodlands have survived all over the Highlands into this century. At present, less than 2% of Scotland is under native woodland cover (SNH Policy Paper *Red Deer and the Natural Heritage*, 1994). Since the Second World War, pressures on these woodlands have become even more severe, despite growing awareness of their increasing rarity. The extraordinary expansion in the number of red deer (and roe deer too now), the increase in sheep, the planting of huge areas of commercial forestry and the depredations of rabbits have all made it more difficult for native woodlands to survive. This has been exacerbated by the perception of landowners that their native woodlands of birch and oak, in particular, amount to no more than scrub and are economically valueless.

By the 1980s, the plight of the native woodlands was apparent. It had resulted from the conflict of land uses arising from the conventional management of hill land for deer stalking, hill sheep farming and commercial afforestation. It is in this context that we may understand the remark in the reserve management plan for Creag Meagaidh of 1987 which was quoted earlier (see page 28) 'At present, grazing impact is nearly maximal. No tree regeneration is taking place except in inaccessible places such as cliff faces or in highly disturbed areas such as road sides.' (NCC Management Plan, 1987).

NCC's plans for regeneration

Having decided that the aim of management of the reserve below the tree line would be to encourage natural regeneration by reducing grazing pressure, the NCC started on a programme of deer culling and the removal of sheep. To measure the progress of the regeneration and other vegetational changes and to provide feedback for management, a monitoring programme was devised. Initially five, and then seven, transects (one kilometre by two metres) were set out[8] and small exclosures made on five of the transects (10 x 10 metre squares surrounded by deer netting). In addition, vegetational cover was estimated in five 2 x 10 metre plots on each transect. These steps

R. BALHARRY

Success!
The forest revives.

have made it possible to monitor changes in the vegetation. Each June the transects are walked – the number of saplings above the height of the surrounding vegetation is recorded and the level of browsing assessed. As the years have passed, the task has taken longer as the pace of regeneration has increased.

The return of the forest

As the chart below shows, changes have happened.....

In 1994, juniper was recorded for the first time, giving an indication of the possibility for change. It is not known how much regeneration is of formerly suppressed saplings that have been able to grow above the height of the surrounding vegetation, and how much is of new saplings that have grown from seed in the last ten years. Fiona Stewart from Aberdeen University is researching this important topic as part of her PhD thesis.

The greatest amount of regeneration is of birch (*Betula pubescens*), but there is plentiful growth of rowan (*Sorbus aucuparius*) and willow (*Salix* spp, but mainly *aurita*) – both notably since 1993. Whereas birch seed is carried by the wind, rowan is distributed by animals, particularly birds, who eat the fruit and

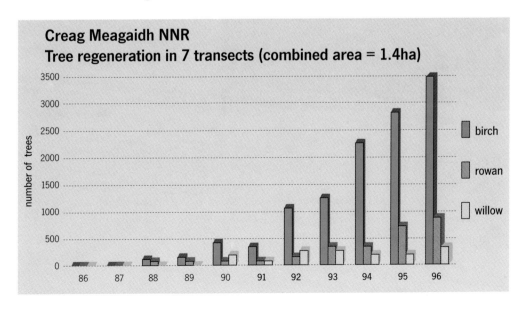

L. GILL

The abundance of regenerating rowan caused some surprise.

to Coire Ardair. Rowan is particularly attractive to deer and its wealth of regeneration is a measure of the reduction of grazing and browsing stock. Other species present, although mainly on Am Meall, include hazel (*Corylus avellana*), oak (*Quercus petraea*), aspen (*Populus tremula*) and alder (*Alnus glutinosa*) along the burn sides (Fry, 1990).

Apart from the reduction in the number of grazing mouths and the erection of the fence around Am Meall, there has been no active management of the vegetational complex at Creag Meagaidh.

Biodiversity and the regenerating forest

The regeneration of the birch woodland and its interaction with the reduced numbers of browsing deer have contributed to the burgeoning diversity of the NNR.

distribute the seeds in their faeces. Often the densest regeneration of rowans at Creag Meagaidh is next to large boulders, favoured perches for passing birds (especially members of the thrush family, such as fieldfares and redwings in the autumn). This is seen very clearly from the path from Aberarder Farm

As the pace of regeneration has speeded up, it has become plain to those who know the reserve that the trees are not the only beneficiaries. Birch and willow are two of the three most abundantly regenerating trees on the reserve at present and they are, with oak, the richest trees in the British flora from the point of view of the number of plant-eating species of invertebrate that they support (Patterson, 1993).[9] The reduction in grazing pressure has also meant that many species of plant, previously apparently present only in relative scarcity, have become more visible. The globe flower (*Trollius europaeus*), grass of Parnassus (*Parnassia palustris*), wood cranesbill (*Geranium sylvaticum*), for example, are able to flower, where previously they were not. The regenerating trees are a developing complex, whose contours are being shaped and influenced by the deer – themselves the biggest biotic influence on the woodland (R Balharry, personal communication). Through most of their range, red deer are animals of the forest edge and of glades within woodland (SNH *Red Deer and the Natural Heritage*, 1994). Roe deer, too, are adaptable creatures of the forest that have learned to live on the open hills of the Highlands as well as in woodland. Each species plays its part in the changing habitat of the growing forest, creating edges and glades. Their nutritional preferences and behavioural characteristics, such as fraying the

L. GILL

Grass of Parnassus.

stems of saplings, help to define habitats for a great diversity of life forms.

R. BALHARRY

A browsing red deer hind prepares herself for the rut and the winter to come.

Deer

The publicity surrounding the acquisition of the National Nature Reserve made it urgent that the number of red deer should be reduced to what the range could sustain, as prescribed in the Management Plan of 1987.[10] It was also important to show that the NCC's management was preferable to the coniferous plantations of Fountain Forestry. In 1985, there were believed to be about 1000 red deer in the NNR (hinds and calves only, according to D Gowans, formerly Head Warden responsible for Creag Meagaidh).

D. GOWANS

Super predators glass the hill.

The neighbours' attitude to the proposed cull

When the NCC's plans to reduce the number of red deer in the NNR became known in 1986, there was consternation among some of the neighbouring estates. Fears were expressed that deer would be drawn into Creag Meagaidh from the surrounding country as the resident deer were killed out, for some were convinced that the NCC was committed to a programme of eradication of deer from the new reserve. Such was the controversy that pressure was put on the NCC and the chairman at the time, Alexander Trotter, called a halt to the cull. However, pressure from non-governmental organisations on the NCC was enough to reverse the decision within ten days, and the cull proceeded as planned (R Balharry, personal communication). Nonetheless, extraordinary hostility was provoked among deer forest owners and also among people who thought (and sometimes still think) that the NCC was hell bent on a policy of mass cervicide. The apprehension of owners of deer forests bordering the NNR was based on the concern that a reduction of red deer on their ground would make it less easy for their stalkers to find the number of deer that stalking clients needed. This perception continues to be a problem elsewhere in the Highlands,[11] despite a general acceptance that numbers of red deer must be reduced in many places.

As the reduction in the numbers of red deer at Creag Meagaidh has been so controversial, it is worth examining the process in detail.

Deer numbers and culling

Table 1 (see Appendix F) shows the number of deer killed from 1985 to 1993, set against the total number of deer on the NNR. The table shows a starting population of 1000 deer on Creag Meagaidh in 1985. A Red Deer Commission census in spring 1977 had given 1200 deer for the forests of Moy and Aberarder and 1300 in 1987, but the count was derived from an area larger than the NNR. The number of stags shot starts with the small figure of two and rises to a peak of 63 in 1987 before levelling off, while the figure for hinds and calves shot starts at 50 and rises to 212 before dropping back. The falling number of deer killed reflects the declining population. The stag cull for each year is agreed with the Monadhliath Deer Management Group, but the number of hinds to be taken depends on a decision

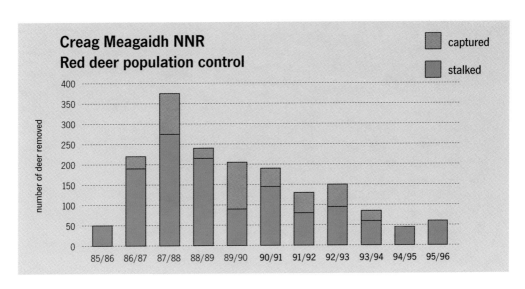

by SNH in the light of natural regeneration of birch and other trees monitored in the reserve. The relatively small number of hinds and calves shot in 1993/4 is a reflection of the availability of animals that winter.

Stalking accounted for nearly three-quarters of all deer culled (i.e. 1200 deer killed out of a total removal of 1666). Over the same period (1985–1993), two-thirds of the hinds and calves removed were shot (897 out of a total of 1363 hinds and calves), while the remainder were removed by live capture.

In 1985, there were about 1000 red deer on Creag Meagaidh ground, but this figure was not a constant one; the numbers then, as now, fluctuating through the year (see table 1 and 2 in Appendix F).

Some hinds return to calve in June and the stags come into the reserve during October. Over the past six years, deer have left the ground from December to April. The reduction in deer numbers means that densities in the reserve have been reduced from 19 per square kilometre or 100 hectares (the average figure for the Monadhliath, according to Red Deer Commission counts in

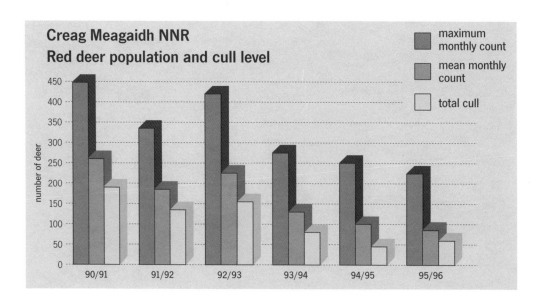

the mid-1980s) to 7.5 per square kilometre in 1993/94. By 1995, the peak monthly counts suggest a density of less than 5 deer per square kilometre. This is the figure at which the late Sir Frank Fraser Darling estimated that deer and regeneration of woodland could co-exist (Darling, 1955). Subsequent research (Holloway, 1967) has confirmed Frank Fraser Darling's intuition, but it would be wrong to apply this figure universally – different situations allow different densities.

R. BALHARRY

Captive hinds in the paddock at Aberarder.

Live capture

The use of live capture was an interesting reversion to a medieval practice. Enclosures into which deer were lured and from which they could not escape were a feature of deer forests of the Middle Ages, and the remains of several survive scattered round Scotland. There are examples at Lintrathen in Angus and near Fettercairn in Kincardineshire (Gilbert, 1979). The decision to capture some deer, rather than reduce the population exclusively by shooting, was made for the following reasons. Firstly, once the catching arrangements had been made, it was much more economical to catch the deer than to go out and shoot them. To put out some turnips, wait for the deer to come into the fenced area and to pull the gate shut was cheap in terms of labour, once the capital costs of fencing had been written off. Secondly, there was a market for wild deer as breeding stock for deer farms in the 1980s. Since then, this market has collapsed owing to the inability of deer farms to compete with heavily subsidised sheep and cattle farming (N Fletcher, personal communication). Live capture also avoided damage to vegetation by all terrain vehicles.

Capturing and handling wild red deer demands patience and a high degree of expertise. Dr John Fletcher, a leading deer farmer in

Scotland and an authority on the welfare of captive deer, advised the NCC on the design of traps and handling procedures. At that time, other estates in Strathspey were also pioneering the practice; they were visited and useful knowledge was gained before the first live catching programme was undertaken.

Once the deer are confined within a perimeter deer fence, they are cajoled with care and patience into the race that leads to the catching pen itself (R Balharry, personal communication). Carried out by experienced staff, using a well-designed trap, the deer remain calm enough for it to be possible to walk among them (P Duncan, personal communication). Wild deer are easier than farmed deer to handle when first caught, tending to freeze when alarmed, which is why they are so quiet in the handling pens. By contrast, farmed deer, being familiar with their surroundings, can be more difficult to handle. Stags are filtered out and released because of the danger to the hinds and calves (J Fletcher and R Balharry, personal communication).

Live capture of hinds and calves over the period from 1985 to 1993/94 has accounted for 27% (449 out of 1666) of all red deer removed from the reserve. The total of hinds and calves removed (including those culled and those taken by live capture) peaked at 308 in 1987/8 and has decreased slowly as the number of deer on the ground has declined. Other advantages of live capture are that the method can be used for selection and to help with research into red deer (by providing deer for tagging, for example). Inevitably, there are some disadvantages, such as the cost of fodder if animals are not sold soon after capture.[12]

R. BALHARRY

July – and a strong red deer calf is troubled by midges.

Territorial behaviour of hinds

Much of the Creag Meagaidh NNR is hind ground, and this fact was critical to the strategy for the reduction of deer and for the plans for woodland regeneration. Red deer, particularly hinds, are strongly territorial and hinds tend to live in family groups of related animals. Research on Rum and elsewhere has shown that herds of hinds are most unwilling to move off ground to which they are hefted (i.e. to which they belong, and specifically where individual hinds were born), even if their own ground is heavily populated or the neighbouring land has few deer or both (Clutton-Brock and Albon, 1989). By reducing the number of hinds within the reserve, hefts are likely to remain unoccupied, at least in the short term.

Two herds of red deer use the land within the NNR, and the limits of the range of each seem to coincide with the historic boundaries of the old forests of Moy and Aberarder. Aberarder deer use Coire Ardair and tend to move back and forth between there and Glenshero, moving in to Coire Ardair at dusk and leaving

R. BALHARRY

Autumn – stag and hind meet in open birch woodland – fit habitat for red deer.

the reserve at dawn. On the west of the NNR, the deer based in the corries of Moy, Coire Meadhonach and the Coire Choille Rais move between these corries and the plateau south and west of Creag Meagaidh itself. The stags that join these groups of hinds and calves are only present on the reserve for five weeks during the rut (Edwin Cross, personal communication).

No sign of a vacuum effect

Culls and censuses show that the number of deer has been reduced greatly since 1985, and the 'vacuum effect' feared by neighbours has not happened. Deer from estates neighbouring Creag Meagaidh do not appear to have moved into the NNR to

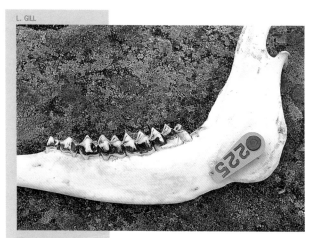

L. GILL

The number of incisors and state of wear of molars are important indicators in assessing the age of deer.

season, three in Braeroy and one in Creag Meagaidh). 1993 was a poor season; the hinds were lean and very few calves were born, only 20 calves being tagged by the RDC. By contrast, in 1994 there was a heavy and early calving. By the time the tagging team got to Braeroy, most calves were too fast to catch, and only three were tagged. 1995 was a good year and 53 calves were tagged, but there have been no returns as yet.

Monitoring

In the early days of the NCC's occupation of the reserve, the priority was to reduce deer numbers and to set up a situation where regeneration of woodland could happen in the presence of deer at lower densities. Unfortunately, it was not possible to monitor enough carcasses. Jaws of culled deer were not removed for examination and a valuable opportunity to study the age structure of the herd was lost. However, recognition of the importance of monitoring as an aid to management resulted in the initiation of a full programme of carcass monitoring in 1992.

The importance of monitoring the red deer on the NNR lies in the

replace those culled, and very few calves tagged on neighbouring estates by the Red Deer Commission have been recorded there (SNH larder records, 1985–1995). To date, only one has been shot. It had been tagged close to the march with Braeroy.

Calf tagging

As part of its monitoring programme, the RDC tagged 146 calves on neighbouring estates (Glen Roy and Glenshero) between June 1992 and June 1995 (86 males and 60 females), but those tagged in June 1992 suffered a heavy mortality. Fifty were tagged that year, but it is likely that few survived the winter of 1992/93 (there were four recoveries in the following hind-shooting information it can yield about numbers, structure of the population (sex ratios, fecundity), recruitment rate, mortality, reproductive status (milk hinds as against yeld hinds) and movements. With such knowledge, it is possible to decide on levels of cull and to predict the demographic consequences arising from a given cull. Carcasses of deer yield much information about the state of individual animals and about the group. Weight and fat cover relate to the state of the range (i.e. the quality of the grazing), as does the weight of antlers. The age of a jaw can be assessed by the stage of tooth eruption and wear, and thus lead to an estimate of the age structure of the herd from which the culled animals came. Details of monitoring requirements for both live and dead deer, including methods and benefits, are given in Appendix B.

Extraction of carcasses

It is sometimes necessary to leave a deer carcass on the hill, if it has fallen in an inaccessible place, for example, but in the great majority of cases carcasses are removed. For the NNR, there is a positive outcome to leaving a carcass on the hill because it exists, in part, to provide a secure habitat for eagles and ravens, and a deer carcass is a sure supply of food for them. However, unless the extraction is going to be too difficult, the aim must be to remove it from the hill. The carcass is both a source of income and food for humans.

Ponies, ATVs and dragging

The change from removing deer carcasses from the hill by pony to the use of an all-terrain vehicle (ATV) is nearly complete

R. BALHARRY

Peter Ross and Duchess bring home a stag.

throughout the country, but there has been a price to pay in terms of damage to vegetation. The creation of unengineered new tracks can lead to unwelcome erosion, causing disagreeable scars in the landscape and often pressure to 'remedy' this by construction of a better track. Such scars are unacceptable and, in a nature reserve, the damage done to vegetation is incompatible with its aims. This has proved to be the case at Creag Meagaidh. With increasing altitude, soils and vegetation become less and less able to bear the pressures that machines impose. Damage that would heal within a couple of years at low altitude can take many years in the subarctic environment above 800 metres. For this reason, the use of ATVs at Creag Meagaidh has been subject to rigorous control.[13] The advantage of an ATV on the hill is its capacity to carry several carcasses and the fact that machines do not tire as men or ponies do, but they are not always reliable, cannot be taken everywhere except at considerable risk to the driver and are expensive to buy and to run. Ponies have the advantage of causing little environmental damage. They do not turn over and crush their drivers and can reproduce themselves. The third choice is to drag carcasses.[14] This is the method favoured by SNH for extraction from relatively low ground. It can be very hard work and carcasses may suffer bruising, which reduces their value.

Helicopters

At times, helicopters have been used to replace extraction by ATV. They were used when it was necessary to extract from inaccessible places and when there were enough carcasses to justify the cost.[15] Of the various methods of removing deer, helicopters have the advantage of damaging the vegetation the least. They cause minimal environmental impact and even their noise can be surprisingly local in its effect. The original intention was to return to the pony and, now that there are fewer deer to cull, one has been acquired from Rum.

Disturbance

It is a common complaint of deer forest owners and their stalkers that walkers disturb deer, putting at risk the achievement of cull targets and jeopardising the satisfactory outcome of a stalk. The feeling of staff at Creag Meagaidh is that visitors affect the success of a stalk beneficially as often as they do adversely, but it does seem that walkers using the path to Coire Ardair make enough disturbance to keep deer away from the immediate vicinity: useful when regeneration of the nearby birchwood is such a high priority.

A survey has shown that many anxieties expressed by the managers of deer forests appear to be unfounded (Staines and Scott,

1992). It is sometimes held that hinds are disturbed at calving to the detriment of the calf. Staines and Scott (1992) found that extraordinarily few walkers ever saw or disturbed a new-born calf and that they very seldom saw newly calved hinds or animals that were about to give birth. Such disturbance as there is does not appear to cause difficulties for the deer, but may result in some alteration of habits. 'On many mainland forests, increased human disturbance of low ground is probably associated with a relative increase in night-time grazing.' (Clutton-Brock and Albon, 1989). So far as management is concerned, the occasional spoilt stalk is frustrating for the stalker, but Staines and Scott (1992) found that most forests they surveyed managed to achieve their cull targets, despite disturbance. This is the case so far at Creag Meagaidh where, despite as heavy a cull as any in the Highlands when deer numbers were high, as many as necessary were shot. Having said that, it is clear that if Creag Meagaidh were a privately owned estate and paying clients were taken out, it could be intolerable for them to have to

L. GILL

Friendly contact between walkers and managers is essential to the smooth running of NNRs and Highland estates.

endure the amount of disturbance that SNH stalkers have to be prepared to accept.

Roe deer and sika deer

Apart from the red deer in the NNR, roe deer that live in the woods of Aberarder are shot within season as necessary. There are also Sika deer (*Cervus nippon*) in the area, particularly to the west of Moy. Within season, these are shot whenever possible to try to prevent hybridisation with red deer, and damage to trees.

Conclusion

The aim of all management of deer carried out at Creag Meagaidh by SNH has been to 'encourage the regeneration and extension of native woodland and scrub vegetation'. The target, as defined in the management plan of 1987 (NCC Management Plan, 1987), was that the deer herd should be reduced to a number at which regeneration measured on sample transects is at least half the level[16] of the regeneration within the fenced woodland of Am Meall (see chart 1 in Appendix F). On this basis, the management has been successful and there is now regeneration in their presence. As the density and distribution of trees increase and the condition of other vegetation improves, it may be possible, in the longer term, to allow deer densities to grow (P Reynolds, personal communication).[17]

Sheep

Sheep have been a problem at Creag Meagaidh ever since it became a NNR. On her native hill, the Blackface ewe is hefted to her own ground: she will return, if she can, to lamb in the place where she was born. At other times, however, she can be an inveterate wanderer, travelling about wherever she may find a fresh bite. Whereas the removal of hinds from Creag Meagaidh has not resulted in significant incursions from elsewhere, the removal of the sheep stock from the reserve has attracted neighbouring sheep. The bar chart on the next page shows the seasonal movement of sheep into Creag Meagaidh over the last ten years.

Grazing by domestic animals is mentioned specifically in the SSSI notification as a potentially damaging operation, so the

L. GILL

A fit looking blackface ewe considers her position.

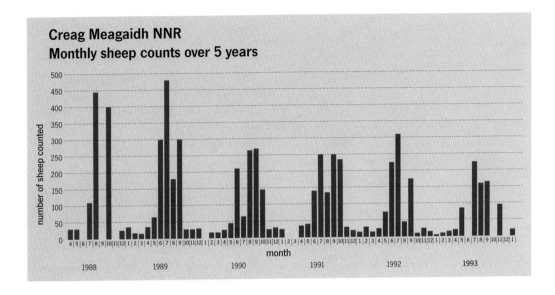

Creag Meagaidh NNR
Monthly sheep counts over 5 years

resolution of the problem of wandering sheep has been particularly important. In the early days of the NNR, the strength of the incursions of sheep from neighbouring estates increased the grazing pressure significantly, even to the extent of doubling it. This threatened to put in jeopardy the point of SNH's efforts to reduce the number of deer. Moreover, the sheep were affecting the composition of the montane heath. The presence of sheep on the higher ground, even relatively few, is now considered to be an even more serious problem than before. This is because of the proposed scheduling of the montane heaths of the reserve as a special area for conservation for their willow scrub, and their nomination as a proposed special protection area under the EU Birds' Directive as a breeding habitat of the dotterel. Whereas deer tend to stay clear of the ledges, sheep are prepared to venture onto them to get at the willow.

The problem of keeping sheep out

The removal of the sheep stock in 1976 resulted in incursions by sheep from the neighbouring estates: Tulloch, Glenshero[18] and Brae Roy. From 1985, it became essential to remove sheep from the NNR and the neighbours have co-operated fully. The shepherd at Glenshero was extremely helpful from the earliest days, but despite frequent gathering and removal of stock (including the selling of ewe lambs born in the Creag Meagaidh area), the sheep returned to Aberarder ground. Accordingly, a management agreement was negotiated with Glenshero over their part of the SSSI, which is outwith the Creag Meagaidh NNR. A condition of the agreement was the erection of a fence on Glenshero ground that excluded sheep from their part of the SSSI, to allow the restoration of habitat. This agreement also prevented sheep from coming into the NNR. Sheep from Braeroy invade the high ground of the reserve during the summer, but at present their numbers are fairly low.

Moving to the west – the Moy dyke has been mentioned. It follows the ancient march between Badenoch and Lochaber and its scale makes it of historical interest as well as a management tool of the present day. Sheep do still come in, but the restoration of the dyke has helped to deflect sheep from the NNR. The dyke is especially effective in winter after sheep have been gathered off the reserve.

However, numbers of sheep are dropping (see figure on previous page), evidence of neighbourly co-operation.

Access

The summit of Creag Meagaidh is famous for its magnificent views. To the east are views of the Cairngorms and to the west of Ben Nevis and its associates. To the north-west Knoydart and beyond that Torridon can be seen in clear weather. Closer at hand are the surrounding hills of the Monadhliath[19] and of the forest of Ben Alder to the south of Loch Laggan. This is a great attraction to many of those who come to the National Nature Reserve; this and the fact that the Creag Meagaidh massif includes three Munros[20] (Creag Meagaidh, Stob Poite Coire Ard and Carn Liath).

Since the 1970s, when modern ice-climbing came of age, increasing numbers of mountaineers have come to exercise their skills on the great cliffs of Coire Ardair (400 metres high and 3 kilometres in extent), which has been described as 'one of the most magnificent and awe-inspiring winter corries in Scotland' (Rawson, 1990).[21] Many new routes have been pioneered, such as the Fly Direct, first ascended by Victor Saunders. The attraction of the cliffs of Coire Ardair to ice climbers results from the way the rocks are bedded, allowing great quantities of snow and ice to build up. A consequence is that avalanches can be spectacular in late winter (Richardson et al., 1994). The significance of winter mountaineering to the numbers of visitors is shown by the high figures for February 1994, a season which was especially good for ice climbing. Although there are ascents of great difficulty, climbs of all winter grades exist. The mountain rescue post by the east end of the Lochan a'Choire, near the foot of the cliffs at Coire Ardair, is a reminder that these cliffs can be dangerous, several fatalities having occurred over the years.

The decade 1985–1995 has seen a steady increase in the number of visitors to the reserve. In 1994, there were 9000, their numbers recorded on the Coire Ardair path by an electronic counter (see chart 2 in Appendix F). The fact that SNH welcomes them means that neighbouring estates can, and do, divert them.

Access has always been an important part of the management of the reserve. The strength of interest in the cliffs of Coire Ardair and the views from the summit of Creag Meagaidh have made it essential that visitors were taken into account from the beginning. So far as the NCC (and now SNH) have been concerned, the management of Creag Meagaidh has created an opportunity to demonstrate how an often controversial problem of land use, that of the interface

G. NICOL

Snow and ice climbing appeal to a growing number of people.

between access by visitors and deer stalking, may be resolved. The conventional view is that disturbance of deer forests by visitors can make it virtually impossible to manage them properly. At Creag Meagaidh, it has been the experience of the last ten

R. BALHARRY

Winter 1986 – on the path to Coire Ardair.

R. BALHARRY

Summer 1994 – from the same place as the top photograph. The light green haze of young birch is visible to the right of the picture.

years that, with no restriction on access and mounting numbers of visitors, it has still been possible to achieve very high culls.

SNH's policy towards casual visitors has been one of minimal intervention, except in the matter of the old stalking path to Coire Ardair. Erosion of the path was a problem from the time of the reserve's acquisition and plans were made to remedy it. A hand-written comment in the margin of the management plan of 1987 (NCC Management Plan, 1987) asks why it should matter if 0.00001% of the reserve is damaged by feet, because the area is so insignificant. However true this may have been in terms of the vegetational interest, there was an undoubted visual impact. Despite its small scale in the great open landscape, the spreading footpath was ugly and not acceptable.

Historically, paths led from one place of habitation to another: they followed trade routes or if they went up hill it was to hill pastures. They tended to go through passes and along sides of glens, where possible, although occasionally, as with the Monega pass from Glen Isla to Deeside, they had to cross high ground.

The urge to climb to the top of hills for recreation dates, for the most part, from the last century as a popular pastime. From that time, new paths began to be made, particularly up the more popular peaks (Aitken, 198-). Since then, increasing access resulting from greater mobility has meant more intense use, and new paths have been formed. These routes often have nothing to do with old paths, at least in the last stages towards the summit. The establishment of the Countryside Commission for Scotland in 1967 meant that there was a body with responsibility for recreation in the countryside and therefore for the development of paths, their construction and maintenance. Arising out of this and the actuality of path erosion in the hills, a new craft of pathmanship has developed. New techniques, such as the laying of old railway sleepers, have been developed, and old skills, such as cobbling and dry-stone dyking, have been revived.

The problem with some forms of new path is that they can detract from the visitor's experience of naturalness. The visitor may feel separated from nature, but it is evident that the trampling of many feet causes erosion, which may become unacceptable, at first visually and eventually environmentally. Decisions at Creag Meagaidh were made with this in mind. Generally, the sleeper path to Coire Ardair has been well received: scarring caused by the installation of the sleepers has healed over quickly.[22] In terms of design, the regularity of the sleeper path, its hard edges and colour are a disadvantage when compared with the more harmonious appearance of paths making use of traditional materials, such as stone (Moore, 1994).

 One disadvantage of the walkway is the greater ease with which visitors can penetrate the heart of the reserve. This may lead to damage to previously less accessible areas; it will be important to continue monitoring the impact of visitors over the years.

Although visitors have enjoyed freedom of access and a right to roam, their dogs have not. Dogs are discouraged, except in the case of guide dogs for the blind and working dogs for the control of sheep. Dog-loving visitors sometimes express annoyance at the rejection of their pets, but the needs of ground-nesting birds, such as the dotterel, must have priority in this special place. The admirable enthusiasms of Munro-bagging dogs must take second place!

Conclusion

This is the background to visitor access at Creag Meagaidh. Visits by schools and other educational institutions are an important part of the programme of countryside education promoted at the reserve. Graphics panels and the presence of captive deer in the park provide points of attention, so that the public may be informed about SNH's policy towards deer. Creag Meagaidh is used to demonstrate the integrated approach to management of the natural heritage enshrined in SNH's duty to further conservation, education and recreation. This is of increasing importance to landowners and managers.

Research, monitoring and surveying at Creag Meagaidh

One of the prime functions of an NNR is 'the study of and research into matters relating to the fauna and flora of Great Britain.....' (National Parks and Access to the Countryside Act 1949). Like its predecessors, SNH undertakes research, which includes surveying and monitoring. Work may be commissioned or it may be undertaken by staff. SNH also permits others to carry out surveys, such as the work on black grouse. Finally, they allow volunteers, like those working at Creag Meagaidh, to undertake their own projects.

Monitoring has been defined as a series of repeated surveys with 'the addition of clear objectives, a precise procedure and rules for when to stop' (Goldsmith, 1993). Ideally, it should provide information on which to base the management of individual sites, as well as contributing to a wider picture with national or international implications. It is about measuring change over time. Current thinking holds that monitoring is part of a process in

L. GILL

Research in action on the NNR.

which objectives are specified for a site, habitat or species. A programme of management is drawn up to make this happen. Finally, the project is monitored to check that management objectives are being achieved (J Matthews, personal communication).

In Appendix C there is a list of all survey work undertaken at Creag Meagaidh since the 1950s and a shorter list (Appendix D) describing the projects. Some of the latter may not fit the Goldsmith rules for monitoring in its narrow sense, but as surveys, they form part of a process of gathering information that has been useful since the acquisition of the NNR. Surveys create a baseline from which trends in distribution and abundance can eventually be discerned. Monitoring, as defined by Goldsmith, is time consuming and expensive, so it is commonly remarked that not enough is done. It is recognised, however, as being increasingly important as we become aware of unexpected environmental changes, including falling numbers of skylarks and thrushes, and some landowners' perceptions about numbers of birds of prey.

At Crèag Meagaidh, the emphasis of monitoring has been on measurement of woodland regeneration (see page 37) and, since 1992, on the red deer population. This form of monitoring is continuous and appears open ended, but the feedback of information makes it possible to assess whether management objectives are being met. Indeed, the challenge is to link results with changes in management to achieve desired outcomes (D B A Thompson, personal communication). Monitoring programmes happen at a number of levels at Creag Meagaidh.[23] That of woodland regeneration is local to the reserve, while that of woodland grouse is part of a project organised by the Game Conservancy and covers a number of sites throughout Scotland. The Montane Ecology Project is a national project run by SNH with a different set of aims.

The Montane Ecology Project – dotterel at Creag Meagaidh

SNH's Montane Ecology Project collected information on a range of subjects to do with Scotland's montane zone, but concentrating on breeding birds, particularly the dotterel (Thompson *et al.*, 1987; Thompson and Whitfield, 1993), which was chosen because of its listing in Annex 1 of the European Union's Bird Directive, and because montane areas that include significant populations of this bird have been proposed as special protection areas (SPAs). The reserve was surveyed for dotterel in 1987, 1988 and 1993, and these surveys showed that it held an important breeding population. This survey work has highlighted many aspects of the distribution and ecology of dotterel unknown before the Montane Ecology Project's work and is an outstanding

D. GOWANS

Dotterel – a rare breeder of the montane zone, the abundance of this species may be an important indicator of climatic change.

and the activities and distribution of grazing animals and predators. However, most effort went into gathering information on the breeding success and choice of habitat of dotterel. The main causes of failure at nesting were found to be trampling of eggs by sheep and loss of eggs due to predation. In terms of their preference for habitat, dotterel in flocks strongly favoured the low-growing carpet of woolly-fringe moss (*Racomitrium lanuginosum*) and stiff sedge (*Carex bigelowii*) heaths, seldom using the relatively tall, dense beds of mat grass (*Nardus stricta*) for nesting.

example of the solid contribution of survey and monitoring to conservation and management, as well as to the development of our understanding of the environment.

Most of the Montane Ecology Project's work was carried out in the Cairngorms and in the east and central Grampians, but in 1993 and 1994 the Creag Meagaidh/Carn Liath plateau was added as a new area of intensive study. Information was collected on a wide range of subjects, including the abundance and activities of people and their dogs,

Dotterel are summer migrants to Scotland and overwinter in north Africa. In contrast with some species that return year after year to the same site to breed, dotterel show relatively low fidelity to breeding and natal site. Some have been recorded as breeding in both Scotland and Norway. Birds, colour ringed or seen on Creag Meagaidh, have added to our picture of the pattern of movements of this species.

Other results of the Montane Ecology Project work included a fuller account of the birds that breed on the Creag Meagaidh/Carn Liath plateau. Information was recorded on ptarmigan, golden plover, dunlin, snipe, wheatears, meadow pipits and skylarks. This mixed bird assemblage reflects the diversity of the montane plant communities, from bog to moss heath on the Creag Meagaidh plateau.

Of birds seen visiting the study area, but not breeding, the most frequent were ravens, golden eagles and hooded crows. The relative abundance of ravens and hooded crows was reversed in the neighbouring lower ground, where hoodies were seen more often than ravens. Merlins, kestrels, peregrines and sparrowhawks were seen occasionally over the higher ground and twite were recorded over the high corries and ridges in spring.

Black grouse

For some years, the black grouse (*Tetrao tetrix*) has been declining nationally (Baines and Hudson, 1995). Indications are that overgrazing by sheep and deer have been important contributory factors. At Creag Meagaidh, Dr David Baines of the Game Conservancy Trust has been monitoring the black grouse. The work is at an early stage, but it is evident that the great increase in the numbers of sawflies and lepidoptera (moths and butterflies) associated with the regenerating habitat[24] has been the source of abundant food for the chicks. In 1995, greyhens on the reserve

reared four chicks each.[25] This represents a potential population increase, because the survival of two chicks until late summer suggests a reasonably static or increasing population the following year. 1995 was a good year for black grouse throughout the country, and the result at Creag Meagaidh was an encouraging sign.

Changes of fauna and flora?

From time to time, concern is expressed that a particular species may be adversely affected by the expansion of the regenerating woodland. Such has been the case with a butterfly, the small mountain ringlet (*Erebia epiphron*), but its range is above the tree line and so it is unlikely to be affected by any expansion of woodland. To date, the experience has been that, so far as is known, the great increase in biodiversity has not been accompanied by the supplanting of open ground species by woodland species of fauna or flora.

A first record

The northern emerald dragonfly (*Somatochlora arctica*) was first recorded in the reserve in 1995. It may be that this species had survived in small numbers on the NNR and, now that the habitat has begun to recover, its presence has risen to a level where it is noticeable. Continued surveying and monitoring will give the answer to this question and many others.

Ferox trout and charr in Loch Laggan

Nothing has been said so far about the Creag Meagaidh experience and freshwater life, but recent research in this field should be described.

Loch Laggan is one of several lochs in Scotland known for their *ferox* trout, a form of brown trout (*Salmo trutta*), which differs from others in being very large and almost wholly fish eating. They occur only in lochs that cover more than 100 hectares and that contain Arctic charr (*Salvelinus alpinus*), which are likely to form the main part of their diet (Maitland and Campbell, 1992).

S. SCOTT

Arctic charr – every loch has a distinctive sub-species.

Recent work by Professor Andrew Ferguson of the Queen's University, Belfast, who sampled the four burns on the reserve by electric fishing, has shown conclusively that there is a relationship between heredity and the production of *ferox* trout. Loch Laggan is the first loch in Scotland for which this connection has been revealed (Ferguson, 1995), although experiments in Norway have shown that piscivorous behaviour can be an inherited characteristic (Maitland and Campbell, 1992).

Conclusion

One of the excitements of the Creag Meagaidh NNR is the enthusiasm with which members of staff describe the happenings there since 1985: the new observations, the recording of first sightings for the reserve and the proliferation of diversity. The results of surveying and monitoring will gradually generate a scientific basis for the impressions of those on the ground. This will create a fund of knowledge on which to base the future management of the reserve and to inform those involved in similar projects elsewhere.

Neighbours

'Guid dykes mak guid neebors'

The forests of Aberarder and Moy are set in more than a context of time and space; there is a social dimension. The anxiety over deer culls and the need to make arrangements for sheep are symptomatic of the need to communicate with neighbours. Bodies such as Scottish Natural Heritage are always in a difficult position. They can often be seen as intruders in a conservative countryside. Strange-seeming goals make the organisation different from more conventional neighbours, whose aims are more easily understood. Environmental conservation and communities in the Highlands have not always been easy associates (Hunter, 1995), but it may be the holistic estate management of the environmental conservationist that has most to offer both Highlander and landowner in the long run. This makes the task of SNH very challenging and makes it more necessary than ever to

L. GILL

Loch Laggan –
looking west.

maintain communications with neighbouring landowners and the community of Laggan.

Misunderstandings can range from the perception that 'scrub', growing where once there was mown or grazed grass, is neglectful or untidy, to questions of management, about which deer and sheep are at the centre. There may also be an element of envy. How can this government organisation throw so much money at a hill just for some scrubby trees and a few birds? It can seem disgraceful to traditional minds that good hill grazings are not being consumed by sheep. All that good meat and nothing to eat it! And then what about the vermin? Do they leave the foxes and hoodies? As a matter of course, there is no control of any so-called vermin on the National Nature Reserve, but if a neighbour complains that a fox has been killing lambs, SNH's staff will co-operate and deal with the problem. In the earlier years of the reserve, some time was spent on the control of foxes at the request of neighbouring estates, but with the exception of 1994, when a lamb was killed at Tulloch, foxes have not been reported as a problem in the area.

This is the reasonable answer, and yet foxes and hoodies are the subject of much emotion. It is often a matter of dealing with this rather than the objective reality of the problem, if such exists, that counts.

Personal contact is important at all levels so, in 1988, it was decided to reactivate the Monadhliath Deer Management Group (A Barton, personal communication). This has proved an essential means of communication through which neighbouring estates can meet to discuss levels of cull and how to put them into effect. At the start of the NCC's tenure, it gave managers from the different estates a chance to air anxieties over the Council's proposals. Currently, it provides opportunities for face-to-face meetings between people whose lives do not allow much time for such activities.

The following piece is written by Richard Sidgwick of West Highland Estates, managing agents for British Alcan at Glenshero.

A view from the other side of the march

As managing agents for Creag Meagaidh's largest neighbour, we watched the developments which took place there during the early and mid-1980s with interest. Before that date, it had formed part of a traditional estate where management objectives were broadly similar to ours at Glenshero and Sherramore but, by the mid-1980s, proposals for large-scale afforestation by Fountain Forestry and the eventual purchase by the NCC indicated that changes were afoot.

L. GILL

Glen Shero – from the roadside past Garvamore.

Shortly after the purchase, NCC staff arranged to meet us to discuss their objectives and, in particular, to establish our reaction to their proposal to make a very significant reduction in deer numbers; at the time, we took the view that this would improve the quality of the grazings to the extent that considerable numbers of both deer and sheep would eventually migrate from Creag Meagaidh's larger neighbours and, although the issue was discussed in detail, our view remained unaltered, whereas that of the NCC was that this would not happen to any great degree.

The position relating to deer movement has been monitored closely over the years, and I am happy to say that our misgivings were unfounded. To date, we have not experienced any noticeable movement in the deer population from Glenshero and Sherramore in a southerly direction into Creag Meagaidh; this is a view which is borne out by the stalkers, and I think that the situation has probably arisen as a combination of the following factors:

1. By comparison with Glenshero and Sherramore (35,000 acres), Creag Meagaidh is relatively modest in size, and the reduction in deer numbers has represented a relatively small proportion of the overall population; if there has been modest movement, then the population at Glenshero has been able to accommodate it without experiencing undue effect.

2. The significant increase in public access over Creag Meagaidh has had an effect on the deer, and I believe that it has a significant part to play in maintaining the Creag Meagaidh population at a low level.

3. Approximately one-third of the Creag Meagaidh march is formed by Loch Laggan and the estate is, therefore, under no pressure from deer in this area; it may well be that if this march was a valley bottom with all the inherent attractions for red deer, then the position may have been different.

who were trying to regenerate birch, but also to the irritation of our shepherds, who were required continually to gather at what is already a busy time of year. This situation has happily been resolved by the conclusion of a management agreement with SNH, which has enabled us to enclose the one remaining hirsel that had free range during the summer months at the same time as excluding sheep from the whole of the Creag Meagaidh SSSI, and the issue is now no longer of significance.

In concluding, I should say that the view from the other side of the march is neither hostile nor suspicious, and that we are more than happy to work with SNH in pursuit of our different objectives.

Conclusion

This is a story about how new owners, with different objectives from those of the past, have set about their aims and have managed, for the most part, to speak to their neighbours, with whose goodwill they have been able to pursue their vision of a sustainable environment.

The situation, insofar as our sheep are concerned, has been more problematic; from an early stage, unenclosed sheep made their way over the march to Creag Meagaidh throughout the summer months, not only to the irritation of the SNH staff

Financial matters

The purpose of this section is to give financial information about the capital and running costs of managing the Creag Meagaidh National Nature Reserve. Comparisons with private estates are hard to make, because the aims of private owners and those of a national nature conservation body tend to differ. SNH is a science-based organisation with responsibility for the care of the natural heritage, particularly areas covered by special designations. This results in a management philosophy that may be very different from the generally pragmatic, conservative or financially driven approaches of traditional estates. All the same, Creag Meagaidh has much in common with a modestly sized Highland sporting property in sharing the need to cull red deer and so the need to employ staff and equipment to achieve this aim. Another characteristic, familiar to many Highland estates, is that, through freedom of access, the community benefits in a way that is significant to the health of the local economy, although bringing no direct financial advantage to the landowner. Finally, it should be remembered that many costs borne to date have been start-up costs, and that income has been temporarily boosted by changes of management. The figures given in this chapter, therefore, should be thought of in the context of a business undergoing change of management, with all the upheavals that may involve, rather than as a going concern.

The consequences of SNH's responsibilities and the objectives of the NNR's management plan also have a bearing on the appearance of the accounts.

Creag Meagaidh was bought for the nation in 1985 for almost £441,000 (£111 per hectare). Since its purchase, three classes of expenditure have been incurred. These are long-term capital costs, such as the walkway and the Moy wall, the need for which has been described previously. Such costs account for projects that have a 'once in a lifetime' character: they tend to be relatively expensive.[26] The second category is shorter-term capital costs (the purchase of equipment that needs to be renewed relatively often, for example, ATVs, radios, etc.).[27] Current expenditure is the third class of expenditure to be found in the accounts. This includes wages and other day-to-day expenses incurred in the management of the reserve offset by any income generated.

Property improvements

The new uses of the reserve, the condition of parts of it and the requirements of Health and Safety legislation made it necessary to undertake certain capital expenditure. This work is largely complete, although, as with any property, further expenditure will be necessary from time to time for improvements to the fabric of the

H. MACKAY

Aberarder Farmhouse
– office of the NNR
and hostel for
researchers and
volunteers.

property. The principal headings of such outlays are buildings and structures, such as the walkway and the car park.

BUILDINGS

A total of £58,900 has been spent on work to buildings at the two steadings on the estate,[28] the main expenditure being the upgrading of the water supply and heating system and the renewal of the windows in the farmhouse at Aberarder. Substantial repair works have also been carried out, including replumbing and rewiring, and improvements to the kitchen, bathrooms and bedrooms. The renovations have made it possible for research workers and volunteers to be housed and to have working facilities during their time at the NNR. They also provide an office for SNH staff. A further £17,500 has been spent restoring the Moy march dyke.

VISITOR FACILITIES

The upgrading of the path to Coire Ardair, already described, cost £44,000. Expensive though this may seem, the price of the work,[29] at just over £29 per metre, was less than that for laying a stone path (about £35 per metre).

This expense was one that the NCC/SNH were bound to incur with their policy of open access, but one which private landowners would be unable to make without considerable assistance from public funds.

The car park below the farmhouse at Aberarder, built for £7500, was also essential as part of the NCC/SNH open-house policy for visitors. As with the pathway, a private estate would have needed public support for such a project.

OTHER CAPITAL COSTS

The second category of capital expenditure is movable equipment,[30] such as vehicles, machinery and equipment at Aberarder, and permanent signs. This has a more readily identifiable annual cost. Since the acquisition of the estate, there has been a total operational capital expenditure of £86,900, with an annual depreciation charge of £9600.

VEHICLES

Two cross-country vehicles were bought. One has been sold, the other, a Glencoe, was kept. It is used for the extraction of deer carcasses, fencing work and for fire prevention. A fire tender was bought for this purpose. In addition, there are a Land Rover, a tractor with a loader shovel and a trailer.

POWER SUPPLY

A total of £16,300 has been spent on improvements to the power supply at Aberarder Farm – the purchase of generators and transverters for the storage of emergency power reserves to support the radio communication system and protect computers in the reserve's office. There is no public electricity supply.

SIGNS

£13,500 has been charged to Creag Meagaidh from SNH's national programme for re-signing all NNRs.

The current account

INCOME

Over the ten years of NCC/SNH management, the largest amount of income has come from venison. Sales totalled £73,000, having fallen from £16,000 per annum and tailed off to £3000. Income from the sale of live deer has followed a broadly similar pattern. Sales peaked at £10,800 in 1990 and totalled £36,000 over the ten years. By 1995, income from the sale of live deer had disappeared and, as long as deer farming is in the doldrums, is unlikely to recover. Venison income from a stable population of deer will continue and, although subject to the vagaries of the market, will probably run at around £4000.

Other income over the ten-year period, totalling some £3400 in respect of rental income from a short-term let of Moy farmhouse and the letting of grazing on the inbye fields, has only come onstream in the last two years. It should be possible to sustain this.

Income has totalled £113,000 over ten years, but the pattern is changing with a shift from deer income, originally the only source of revenue, to a slightly broader base, although at a level of around £5000, unless the letting of stalking is introduced.

EXPENDITURE – STAFF

Costs for a warden and latterly two estate workers as well as a share (10–20%) of SNH's area officer have totalled £370,000. Annual costs have increased from just under £28,000 in 1985 to £62,000 in 1995. Over the last ten years, the red deer cull has been the single activity that has taken up most time. Half of this is accounted for by stalking and one-third has been associated with live capture and management of the captive herd. As numbers of deer have diminished, they have become more alert and difficult to shoot and increased effort is needed per deer to achieve the required cull. Labour costs do not necessarily drop with decreasing numbers of deer.

RED DEER

Direct costs of managing the red deer, including the erection of fencing,[31] have amounted to £57,500 over the period, but with catching facilities built and the captive herd diminished, future cost levels for these two items should diminish significantly.

OTHER COSTS

With a backlog of work to be undertaken, building repairs totalled £47,500, and general estate maintenance, including tools, fencing materials, etc., came to a further £42,400. The annual cost of these two items should also decrease by around a half to some £3500–4500. Sundry costs relating to vehicles, visitor management (£500 per annum), office and research expenses and radio costs have totalled £22,800 over the ten years. They are expected to continue slightly above this level at between £2500 and £3000 a year.

RADIO

In common with many other estates, a greater awareness of health and safety at work, coupled with advances in technology, has resulted in the installation of a radio communication system. This has many benefits for staff working on the reserve and for communication with the Strathspey office. As many stalkers will be aware, the use of radio helps with efficient recovery of deer carcasses, with co-ordination during the stalking season and with deer counts. It has also proved invaluable in alerting mountain rescue teams when human lives have been in danger (R Balharry, personal communication).

SUMMARY

The current account deficit has risen from £30,000 per annum over the first five years to £80,000 in the last three years and has totalled £439,000 (equivalent to just over £11 per hectare a year). A further £215,000 of capital expenditure has been incurred with an aggregate depreciation charge of £53,750 to date. Thus, one measure of the average annual running costs of the reserve over this period would be £49,275 (£12.50 per hectare). The net spend over the same period gives an annual average of £65,400 (£16.50 per hectare). Now that the distortions of the early years are largely past, and with some £125,500 of the capital spend capable of being regarded as a long-term investment with no recurring annual cost, it is reasonable to envisage a normalised annual running cost of roughly the same order. With a net current account deficit of some £54,000 and an annual depreciation charge on short-term capital items of £10,000, the running cost would be £64,000 (£16.20 per hectare).

EMPLOYMENT

At the time that Fountain Forestry wished to plant the ground they had bought from Loch Laggan Estates, they claimed that six men would be employed in the planting of trees. These men would probably have been made redundant after planting had been completed. Thereafter, during the establishment phase, a squad would have come in once a year for a few days to do any necessary beating up and weeding. From the establishment of the plantation five years after completion of planting until its thirtieth year, there would have been little need for labour in the forest with only occasional visits necessary to carry out maintenance of ditches and fences over the following five or ten years.

In contrast, the NCC started by employing one full-time man and one part-time. By 1993, the part-timer had become full time and by 1994[32] another part-timer, who had been taken on in 1991, was working full time.

Conclusion

The case is made that for a relatively small cost (£16 per hectare per annum[33]) the NNR is managed for conservation, recreation, research and education. £300,000 has been estimated to return to the local economy in the period of time since the acquisition of the estate (Moore, 1994). As part of the management for conservation, diversity of habitat and species are being protected, native woodland is regenerating successfully and the biological capital of the area is being enhanced. Unfortunately, no-one has yet devised a way of accounting for environmental capital in a balance sheet, but if they had the figures would look good.

A decade of management – conclusions

The decade ends with the new management plan for the reserve, which describes the long-term objectives. These were 'to secure the conservation and enhancement of the natural heritage between loch shore and the summit of Creag Meagaidh', and 'to promote public appreciation and enjoyment of the area consistent with the first aim and to promote the reserve for demonstration purposes'[34] (SNH, 1995).

During the decade since Creag Meagaidh was acquired, the qualities that made the reserve important at the outset have been confirmed and extended. Difficult decisions had to be taken about red deer, but their implementation was followed by a magnificent regeneration of the birch woodland. Despite one of the heaviest deer-culling programmes in the country, a policy of open access for visitors was followed throughout. Some lessons that were drawn from this experience are the subject of the next chapter.

[1] There is no mention of Creag Meagaidh in the great *Oran na Comhachaig* (probably composed late in the sixteenth century) by the Lochaber poet Domhnall Mac Fhionnlaidh nan Dan. In that famous evocation of the Gaelic landscape, Ben Nevis, Fersit, Loch Treig, Ben Alder, Insch, Daviot and many other places in the central Highlands are mentioned, but not Creag Meagaidh. Nor is Creag Meagaidh mentioned in the Reverend Thomas Sinton's *Poetry of Badenoch*.

[2] During the Middle Ages, the royal deer forests gradually passed into agriculture and eventually to private ownership (Gilbert, 1979). By 1811, there were said to have been only six deer forests in the land (Glenartney, the Blackmount, Mar, Invercauld, Glen Fiddich and Atholl) (Hart-Davies, 1978), although deer did survive elsewhere (else how would Rob Donn have worked as a stalker in the Reay Forest?). In the 1750s, the poet and deer stalker, Donnchadh Ban Mac an t-saoir, complained in his *Cumha Coire Cheathaich* (*Lament for Coire Cheathaich*) that the sheep, which had been introduced by the Breadalbane Estate into Glen Lochay, had driven out the deer and degraded the range (MacLeod, 1952).

[3] The 'vacuum effect' is the term given to the notion that deer, particularly hinds, will move in and colonise an area of ground on which the numbers of resident deer have either been reduced, or from which they have been cleared.

[4] Although it has to be borne in mind that the RSPB have begun to kill foxes and crows as part of a five-year experiment into the productivity of woodland grouse, at much the same time as they have started to take down deer fences.

[5] The maximum tree line was probably reached by 8000–7000 BP (Birks *et al.*, 1988).

[6] Authorities vary as to how much of the country was wooded. Smout says 50–60% in his *Scotland since Prehistory* (1993).

[7] There are those who question the assumption that moorlands have arisen predominantly from burning or felling (or both) of ancient woodland rather than from grazing (Thompson and Miles, 1995).

[8] A transect is a line on the ground drawn from one place to another and chosen by a statistically validated process to be random. Having chosen a transect by this method, the ecologist then surveys the vegetation (in this case) along the line and records it. At intervals of time the transect is resurveyed and any changes noted.

[9] Willow is first with 450 spp., oak next with 420 and birch third with 350.

[10] The Monadhliath was, according to the RDC's counts, one of the most densely populated areas of the Highlands (Clutton-Brock and Albon, 1989).

[11] Although not at Glenshero. For the reason why, see the section on neighbours.

[12] During the 1980s, live-caught hinds were worth a premium as breeding stock; an increased value which helped the economics of running the reserve (P Duncan, personal communication).

[13] See Appendix E. SNH intends to write a guide to the use of ATVs on land in the hills.

[14] But new regulations about the handling of weights over 25 kg may be relevant to this method of extraction in future.

[15] The cost of helicopters for the extraction of deer carcasses at Creag Meagaidh was raised in the House of Lords by Lord Burton in February 1988 (Hansard).

[16] As measured by the number of saplings above the height of the surrounding vegetation.

[17] Particularly if the sex ratio is kept close to 1:1.

[18] Glenshero is spelt in a number of ways – Glenshirra Forest according to the Ordnance Survey's 1:50,000 map, Glen Shero, Glen Shiaro (Sinton, 1910). Watson spells it Shiara in his authoritative *History of the Celtic Place Names of Scotland*, first published in 1926, and gives it the meaning 'lasting river' – see Appendix B).

[19] The word means 'grey moorland or mountain range' and contrasts with Monadh Ruadh – red moorland or mountain range, the Gaelic name for the Cairngorm massif.

[20] A mountain of 3000 feet and more, named after an Angus landowner and mountaineer, Sir Hugh Munro of Lindertis, who listed all the hills of 3000 feet and over in Scotland. The Revd A E Robertson, for many years Minister of Rannoch, was the first to climb all the Munros.

[21] And in particular, the striking 'posts', which give the central section of the cliff its name of the 'postface'.

[22] The low cost of maintenance was also a big advantage of using sleepers (P Duncan, personal communication).

[23] A countryside management system (a relational database) is now in use at Creag Meagaidh and will become increasingly important in the management of the reserve.

[24] Birch and the vegetational mosaics of the forest floor.

[25] There were six greyhens within the count area – extrapolating to the rest of the available habitat, there were probably as many as 20 to 30 (D Baines, personal communication).

[26] Some may legitimately be regarded as not having an annual cost – i.e. the cost is written off to capital in the year of expenditure.

[27] These are costs to which it is relatively easy to impute an annual cost.

[28] All but about £2500 of this was for long-term improvements.

[29] The complete length of the path from Aberarder to Coire Ardair is 5.5 kilometres, but the length of sleeper-laid path amounts to 1.5 kilometres.

[30] That is, more rapidly depreciating equipment.

[31] This accounts for almost half of the sum in question.

[32] To put this in context, it is interesting to note that the recent Nautilus study carried out for SNH has shown that commercial forestry is a considerably better employer than are sporting estates or hill sheep farming (Nautilus Consultants, 1995).

[33] This figure takes into account the figure derived from subtracting income from expenditure and includes annualised depreciation on short-term capital. It leaves out long-term capital.

[34] The management objectives of the 1995 Management Plan for Creag Meagaidh NNR are to be found in Appendix G.

CHAPTER IV: THE RELEVANCE OF THE CREAG MEAGAIDH EXPERIENCE

Introduction

The last chapter will have given the reader some idea of the management of the Creag Meagaidh NNR over the last ten years. The aims, as described in the 1987 Management Plan, were principally to promote naturalness, with the intention of building up environmental capital. Progress is being made within the strict terms of Scottish Natural Heritage's legal responsibilities, but a constant thread that runs through this account of the Creag Meagaidh experience, and similarly throughout the history of environmental conservation in the Highlands, is the link between the conservation of nature and the experience of management of the wider landscape. The subject of this chapter is to consider what relevance this may have for those who are involved in the management of Highland estates. Over the past ten years, the pressure on the hills caused by growing numbers of red deer, the consequences of 50 years of commercial forestry, the loss of wintering grounds to hydro-electric schemes and their effect on grazing densities of deer and sheep, together with pressing questions of access to the countryside have all become more important to land managers, as well as to conservationists. The experience of SNH at Creag Meagaidh has much to contribute to the discussion about these increasingly urgent matters.

Wilderness and plenty

Creag Meagaidh is relevant to environmental and land use resource conservationists as an example of a land which, having reached a low point in degradation (Darling, 1955; McVean and Lockie, 1969), has nevertheless been able to respond abundantly to a conservation programme. In terms of land use, the NNR may be seen as part of a pattern, a place to demonstrate how the pursuit of a different land ethic may result in practical benefit. In recent times, most private landowners in the Highlands have been unable or unwilling to try the imaginative, bold, pioneering approaches that are necessary to get us out of the morass of unsustainable land use in which we find ourselves.[1] There is a place in land management for research and development, and this is where Creag Meagaidh finds itself as part of a pioneering approach of growing relevance to the wider landscape of the Highlands.

Sir John Lister-Kaye has written of tracts of the Highlands that seem, through mismanagement due to overgrazing and overburning, to be reduced to 'miles and miles of bugger all – MAMBA' (Lister-Kaye,

73

1994). The revisionist reply that perhaps that is all there would be anyway is falsified by the evidence from Creag Meagaidh, the work of such as Miles (1988) and the evidence of many disturbed sites throughout the country where woodland returns, whenever it is given the chance (Peterken, 1993). Wherever sources of viable seed and suitable soil conditions coincide, there is the potential for natural regeneration of woodland up to and beyond the present tree line. This is not to say that there are not stretches of land where climatic and other contributory circumstances have led to the formation of blanket bog and, thus, an edaphic climax; an appropriate end point. The ultimate goal is the re-establishment of a mosaic of dynamic habitats of which woodland is a part.

Landowners

Apart from ecologists and conservationists, the main body of people for whom Creag Meagaidh is relevant must be landowners, their managers and advisers and, as questions of sustainable land use develop, there is a political dimension.

R. BALHARRY

May 1993 – the regeneration of birch is getting under way.

R. BALHARRY

July 1996 – same place, but allowing for the different time of year, note the change – look back to the chart on page 37.

There is no such thing as a typical Highland estate, nor is there a typical Highland landowner. It is also the case that estates are owned by entities other than individuals. These include joint owners, trusts and companies (Armstrong and Mather, 1983) – among which one should number investment forestry companies. Generalisations, however, have to be made and Highland landowners and their estates are not so idiosyncratic and dissimilar one from another as to nullify anything that might be said about them collectively. A first category of Highland landowner would be one for whom the estate is home and a resource from which a living has to be made to survive. A second category would be one for whom the estate is a holiday home. The first may have sufficient financial resources with which to fund the estate, but is often struggling, rich in land but poor in liquidity. The owners stay because they have inherited the land and want it to stay in the family. Their way of life is valued. A factor in the 'holiday home' owner's tenure will be that he or she is rich enough to bear the losses of the estate. It does not need to be profitable, but very few people like their pleasure to cost too much.[2] This means that, when much is made of the fact that few sporting estates do not lose money, the rich owner may think that this is bearable, would be astonished that anyone thought otherwise, and would suggest that no one who was not rich enough should contemplate the luxury of owning such a property. So far as this proprietor is concerned, an important consideration may be the hoped-for capital appreciation when the time comes to sell. This is important in considering which activity at Creag Meagaidh might have some relevance to a landowner, particularly if there are financial inducements for the regeneration of habitat by the removal of sheep, for example. The rich proprietor might be quite unmoved, believing the Highlands are fine as he finds them and there is no reason for change. A survey of grouse moor owners in 1989 by McGilvray and Perman (1991) found that 60% did not wish for any change. However, having said that many landowners were not much concerned with restoration of habitat, many are now becoming more so as the convergence of interests is better appreciated. The decline of the grouse, the comprehension, at last, that there are too many deer in large parts of the Highlands, the loss of salmon in the rivers, and the consequent recognition that land management in upland areas of the catchment may be at least partly involved in the whole problem, are all leading landowners to reconsider their position. This changing understanding is made plain in the paper delivered to the Standing Conference on Countryside Sports by Graeme Gordon, Convener of the Scottish Landowners' Federation in October 1995 (Gordon, 1995). Similarly, the conference held in Inverness on 20 October 1995 by the Royal Society for the Protection for Birds and the British Deer Society was interesting because the landowners present showed a much greater awareness of environmental degradation than had appeared to be the case before and seemed to agree in this perception with the conservationists, one even quoting the words of Sir Frank Fraser Darling with approval (Pearson of Rannoch, 1995). The fact that the RSPB and the BDS were able to hold a conference together at all showed how far relations have changed between conservationists and an important sector of the Highland land use scene.

Armstrong and Mather's paper about landownership in the Highlands, published in 1983, showed that land changed hands remarkably often. In the west Highlands, they found that only four estates had remained in the same family's hands for more than 100 years. About 6% of Highland estates changed hands every year in the period of their study, compared with 2% for the rest of Scotland. A beneficial aspect of this rapid turnover has been the creation of opportunities for

L. GILL

A croft at Clashmore on the North Assynt estate, Sutherland, where the crofters bought their land.

green charities, who have been able to buy land to manage for its wilderness qualities. The RSPB, the John Muir Trust, the National Trust for Scotland and others have become landowners, or extended their holdings in the Highlands, with sometimes very different aims from those of recent tradition. These bodies have been able to benefit directly from the expertise gained by SNH in the management of Creag Meagaidh and other reserves. SNH's experience at Creag Meagaidh is also relevant for the people of Laggan and elsewhere in the Highlands, where communities (especially crofting communities) are taking opportunities to acquire land and woodland to manage and to hold.

Valuation

Landowners, particularly those who see their Highland estate as a temporary venture, look to the capital appreciation of their property as the offset for the expenditure that they have made on it during their tenure. The valuation of Highland sporting estates is done on the basis of the numbers of game animals and fish that can be expected on past performance to come from it. There may also be an added amenity value, or heritage element, for especially attractive countryside or an interesting house. This is hard to assess in financial terms, so the valuer focuses on the known commodity that people come to shoot or catch.

Conservation blight and conservation boon chase each other as ideas through the valuer's mind as he tries to assess an estate's worth. Thus, a red deer stag is valued at £15–20,000, a brace of grouse at £1000–2500 and a salmon at £2000–4000 on a less-known river or £6000–8000 on one of the better known (Egdell, 1995 and D Gwyther, personal communication). In these terms, anything that suggests reducing the numbers of valuable game will reduce the amount that a prospective buyer will be prepared to pay. The prospect of losing the capital appreciation is an unpleasant one to an owner who is about to sell. However, the decline of the grouse moors over so much of the country and the problems of the salmon are encouraging landowners to consider new approaches, as are woodland grant schemes, such as the New Native Pinewood Scheme.

The tale of the Arabian prince who wondered if his jumbo jet would be able to land at a certain county town's small airport is not apocryphal. Highland sporting estates are globally recognised assets – rewards and symbols of status and success to individuals who have made it in the world marketplace. Appeals to the pockets of owners such as these are not likely to be heard, but an approach that relates to an idea of stewardship, which incorporates enhancement of biological capital, may be more rewarding in the long run, particularly if reinforced by able professional advice.

The land managers

Key figures in the formulation of policy and implementation of decisions about estate management are the factors, professionals with cross-disciplinary expertise in the management of land. Their training and experience include the technical and economic aspects of agriculture, forestry and planning. Up to the present time, the emphasis of this training has been on the economics of estate management and has not included much ecological background. This means that many factors may be unaware of the ecological principles underlying the sustainable management of land, although some individuals do have a background and interest in the environmental sciences. Added to this lack of ecological background is an equivocal position on their place in the carrying out of important decisions with long-term consequences for land use.

R. BALHARRY

A group of land owners and managers (and others) visits the NNR.

Shooting possibilities resulting from a move to woodland

Heather moorland is a seral stage. In terms of the plant succession, of which it is part, it may be moving towards woodland; initially birch, but eventually possibly forest dominated by oak or pine. The experience at Creag Meagaidh is that, in a situation of such vegetational instability, it may be better to let the succession run and benefit from the range of birds and animals there, in sporting terms, rather than try to keep the simple heathland that is difficult and expensive to manage. A relatively small sporting estate of the kind that Creag Meagaidh would be, if in private hands, might provide a more diverse fauna, although with smaller bags for the sportsman, than a larger area of more rigidly managed vegetation. This does not mean that there is no place for the intensively managed grouse moor: there may be in the eastern Highlands, particularly if the standards proposed by John Phillips and Adam Watson can be applied (Phillips and Watson, 1995); but it is to be wondered whether present trends can be reversed, especially given the shortage of labour in the countryside for well-controlled burning. Protagonists of heather moorland advance its case by saying that it is the last resort of a range of birds and mammals that depend on it. That argument has recently been dented by evidence that, apart from the red grouse, few other birds are solely dependent on intensively managed heather moor (Brown and Bainbridge, 1995). Finally, the outlook for heather moorland, if it is unable to resist the cumulative effects of acid rain, may be poor, and for that reason conversion to birchwood with its tendency to reduce the acidity of soils may have an important part to play in buffering the effects of this form of aerial pollution. Once again, the experience at Creag Meagaidh has a relevance to the wider world of land management.

Deer and deer stalking

The primary relevance of the experience at Creag Meagaidh in relation to deer stalking has been to confirm that the so-called 'vacuum effect' has not operated there. This lends support to experiences in Rum, Inshriach and elsewhere (Clutton-Brock and Albon, 1989). Unfortunately, it is not yet possible to make any statements about the benefits to a deer manager that can accrue from keeping the red deer in a forest to a number that is well within the limits of the carrying capacity.

The figures given for deer on the Aberarder and Moy ground, both annually and through the years, give snapshots: deer move back and forth through the Monadhliath and this depends on season, weather and disturbance. The stag that ruts in Coire Ardair may have come across from Glenshero or elsewhere. The hinds that drop their calves in Coire Moy may have come in from Brae Roy. More needs to be known about the movements of the deer through the seasons and this gives strength to the feeling that more use will need to be made of local management groups to consider matters beyond the setting of culls.

The number of red deer on the NNR has been reduced from 19 to about 5 per 100 hectares (SNH monthly counts). This has been taken to be a density at which regeneration of woodland can prosper. Some of the unease felt by owners of deer forests, when they are told by experts that they should reduce the numbers of deer, is due to the fact that they wonder how they will be able to continue to employ a stalker with fewer deer. Before they reach that point, there is the period of time during which the numbers of deer are being reduced. How will the stalkers manage to shoot as many deer as may be necessary, given the restrictions of season, weather, an increasingly alert herd of deer and the reality of disturbance by walkers? In addition, there is the fact that part of the problem in the Highlands is the frequently considerable imbalance of the

L. CAMPBELL

Better habitat means better beasts. A fine royal guards his harem of hinds.

sexes. Whereas there was thought to be one stag for every 1.3 hinds 20 years ago, there is now a sex ratio of one stag to two hinds in many places (Red Deer Commission Annual Reports). The more hinds there are relative to stags, the greater the initial reproductive potential of the herd,[3] so it is no surprise to learn that there has been a doubling of deer numbers in the eastern Highlands in the last 20 years. Although there is a problem, there is room for manoeuvre. Hinds are the important target of the reduction and it may be that stags do not have to be reduced by more than a little. This is the experience at Creag Meagaidh where the overwhelming weight of the stalkers' efforts (and the live catching paddock) has concentrated on achieving a heavy cull of hinds and calves. This itself brings an increased monetary reward in the gap before a regime of slightly fewer stags of greater weights and larger antlers[4] comes into play.

Some work has been done with modelling techniques to show how a relatively small population of deer may produce enough shootable stags. The aim would be to give a return of much the same amount of money with fewer deer than a conventionally managed estate would previously have brought in with more (Clutton-Brock and Lonergan, 1994; Buckland et al., 1996).[5] Models can be dangerous things because, although their makers always insist that they can only be used as a guide, those who do follow the courses of action that they suggest (or tell others to follow) often follow them to the letter.

Clutton-Brock and Albon (1989) and Clutton-Brock and Lonergan (1994) have shown that, in situations where females are lightly culled and predominate in the adult population, managers should be able to increase both the number and quality of mature males taken each year by culling more females as a proportion of the population; this follows from the fact that high densities of hinds are associated with a deterioration of body performance among stags, as well as greater mortality and emigration of males. There are other reasons, also, why a loss of stag stalking is unlikely to happen. Stalking, rather than culling, is related to the number of beats, stalkers and days available, rather than the total population size. For example, in three estates in the central Cairngorms, the stag cull is the same as it was in 1967; yet the deer stock has doubled. The same stalking could be achieved, therefore, with half, if not less than half, of the current population (SNH, 1994).

A point that is sometimes made during visits to the NNR by deer forest owners and managers is that the successful regeneration of the woodland will result in the loss of a unique form of field sport. The counter to this argument is that there will always be enough land above any conceivable tree line to leave sufficient open ground for this form of stalking and that new skills will be developed, familiar to those with experience of deer stalking in woodlands on the mainland of Europe and elsewhere in the world. Variety will thus be enhanced.

Animal welfare is an important factor in deer management, particularly as large culls to contain excessive numbers are taken. The experience at Creag Meagaidh is that this sensitive area has to be taken seriously. Stalkers need to be well trained in the basics of their craft, but also in its public relations aspects. Estates have to become more aware of public relations skills and the presentation of arguments. A retreat to tradition is not possible.

Access

Access has become increasingly a question in the Highlands as numbers of visitors to the area have grown. The *de facto* right to roam of the past has become more difficult for some private estates to accept, particularly as land falls into the hands of new owners from outside Scotland who do not understand old tradition. At Creag Meagaidh it has been possible to achieve the high culls of deer that were necessary in the presence of visitors, because a professional stalker is on his own there or with other skilled people. On the other hand, it is doubtful if a private estate that depended on income from rents for the actual stalking could stand the disturbance. Owners of deer forests perceive that there is more disturbance of their activities in the

hills, since hill walking has become more popular. Equally, walkers often feel that their customary right to be in a particular place is being compromised by stalking. At Creag Meagaidh, the policy of open access means that staff are especially conscious of the need to take the public into their confidence and to explain what they are doing, so that the visitor can understand the relevance of the stalker's activity.

Over the years the intensity of the cull at Creag Meagaidh has made the deer very wary. Stags are less alert than hinds, but beasts that would be approachable on many deer forests, where the intensity of culling has been less, are extremely hard to get close enough to to shoot. Culling pressure is the greatest disturbance in a deer forest; and the greater the pressure, the more difficult it becomes to achieve the aims of any management plan. Access may spoil the shooting of a particular stag, but it has not, so far, been shown to prevent the achievement of annual culls. Estates that were approached by Professor Staines in his preliminary study of public access and deer management found that, despite disturbance, they managed to get rifles to their quarry sufficiently often. Nor has public access been shown to disturb hinds at and around calving unduly (Staines and Scott, 1992). This is important because woodland regeneration projects only attract maximum grants if landowners are prepared to encourage access (see Appendix H).

HIGHLAND BIRCHWOODS

A mobile saw bench converts birch into saw logs.

A different kind of forestry

For the last 50 years, there has been a continuous change in attitudes towards forestry. The process can be recognised in the changes that have taken place in the system of grants. Formerly directed towards the establishment of coniferous woodlands, they are redirected now to encourage the planting of broad-leaved woodlands and pinewoods of native provenance. Furthermore, natural regeneration has come into its own with favourable terms. Such was the case with the Woodland Grant Scheme 2, introduced in 1991 (replacing WGS1), and replaced by WGS3 in 1994.

There have been a number of other important developments in forestry. Firstly, the Crofter Forestry Act has opened the way for regeneration and planting on common grazings.[6] Creag Meagaidh will be a good example of what can be done and will support and encourage others, but in many places there is already regeneration of forest. The Forestry Authority (FA) has paid grants to help with the regeneration of 4000 hectares of native woodlands in the 1995/96 financial year already, not all on large estates.[7] Secondly, the Farm Woodland Premium Scheme, combined with WGS, has proved attractive to many small farmers in the north, and the FA has introduced a Livestock Exclusion Premium under WGS3 to compensate for loss of grazing within semi-natural woodlands. Payments under WGS3 may in some cases be less but they are much better targeted than under the provisions of WGS2 (R Dunsmore, personal communication). 'On ancient woodland sites, the regeneration of appropriate native species after a commercial crop can be a positive land use change and on some sites, which are marginal for commercial forestry, native woodland regeneration or planting may be a much better alternative than replanting with a marginal commercial crop' (R Dunsmore, personal communication). This potential goes beyond restock sites to regeneration on the open hill. The provision of WGS supplements for environmentally beneficial management expenditure and the loss of tax relief for management costs, which encouraged more intensive silvicultural practice, offers landowners and community-based rural development foresters, such as crofters, the real possibility of going in for what has been pioneered at Creag Meagaidh.

Financial returns from birchwoods

The possibility of using native birchwoods as a lower input form of forestry is gaining interest for they have the potential to produce timber of saw-log quality in woodland that retains high environmental and social benefits. As the area covered by managed birch forest increases, such problems as volume and quality of supply will be resolved and new markets developed. The real opportunities for the silviculture of birch for economic timber production lie at lower altitudes than the Creag Meagaidh NNR and on better soils, but it is interesting to note that, even in relatively unfavourable situations as at Creag Meagaidh, there are possibilities.

Birch has been a much neglected timber in this country. Pioneering work on silvicultural techniques suitable for birchwoods and in market research has been done by Highland Birchwoods, but it will take time for this to yield results. Birch has diverse uses, from the flooring and furniture that can be made from its saw logs to the food and pharmaceutical products that can be derived from its leaves, bark and sap. Timber production, although likely to be the most important source of income from a birchwood, should only ever be regarded as one component of the series of products that may be derived from native woodland management. Management to maximise timber production might generate a higher proportion of good saw logs, but would be inappropriate in the context of a NNR.

The Forestry Authority's Woodland Grant Scheme and Creag Meagaidh

The success of woodland regeneration at Creag Meagaidh led SNH to consider whether it would qualify for the Forestry Commission's woodland regeneration grant if it were a private landowner.[8] Tilhill Economic Forestry was contracted to carry out an environmental assessment on the reserve, as this would be needed to support a WGS application on such a scale. The report confirmed that SNH's activities at Creag Meagaidh were not damaging the ecological value of the area and that this could make the organisation eligible for WGS3's natural regeneration option. A draft WGS application was prepared to give an example of what might happen if SNH were a private owner who wished to enter the Woodland Grant Scheme and apply for the regeneration option. SNH's example in this particular project is directly relevant to private landowners worried about the degradation of habitat on their estates. If the FA has accepted that enough regeneration of woodland would occur without a fence, SNH would have been off to a good start with a woodland that, in private or community hands, could be managed with some commercial aims as well as for the enhancement of a landscape. Such woodland, moreover, would enhance sporting estates. A summary of the woodland regeneration scheme is to be found in Appendix H.

If continuity of grant were to be assured, together with clarity of purpose and properly agreed programmes of management with the FA, there would be little doubt that many landowners would be happy to make long-term commitments to schemes of the kind just described for Creag Meagaidh.

Conclusion

The relevance of the experience of Creag Meagaidh over the past ten years, in the narrow sense, is that SNH has shown that, by cutting numbers of deer, regeneration of woodland can occur, bringing with it greatly increased biodiversity, and that this can happen in the presence of people. In the wider countryside, Creag Meagaidh has played a pioneering part in the changing estimation of native woodlands as a resource with high environmental and social benefits. These things are directly relevant to landowners and managers.

[1] It is not a new idea to suggest that the land uses to which the Highlands have been exposed are unsatisfactory. From 1879, there were complaints that excessive sheeping of the Highlands was resulting in a loss of fertility, and the

substitution of Blackface sheep for Cheviots was cited as indicative of a loss of grazing quality (Roberts, 1879 quoted by Mather in Smout, 1993). The loss of native forest, sometimes attributed in folklore to the depredations of the Vikings and more recently, on stronger evidence, to burning and grazing (Gimingham, 1995), has been seen as indicative of environmental degradation. Similarly, the recent decline in the number of grouse (including black grouse and capercailzie) and salmon has been seen as being associated with indications of environmental mismanagement. So far as sheep are concerned, most of the historical evidence for these claims has been circumstantial and impossible to substantiate (A S Mather in Smout, 1993). It is clear, too, that salmon numbers have fluctuated considerably since records were first kept, up to 200 years ago, and that these fluctuations of catch may be due to weather, human effort, etc. (Summers in Smout, 1993) and have little to do with environmental mismanagement. It is the case, however, that Scotland is in a boreal forest zone and that, wherever it can, forest returns to take over the land up to a variable tree line (Miles, 1988). Moreover, work, such as that of Miles, has compared open moorland with neighbouring birch woodland on equivalent sites, and this has shown qualitative differences in soil fertility. Under woodland, soils tend to be less acidic, more biotically active and diverse in their flora and fauna (Miles, 1985). Given that most heather sites below the natural tree line were once woodland, there is a clear presumption of decline, and this supports the case that removal of the tree cover, grazing and burning have led to a deterioration of the ecological wealth of the Highlands.

[2] On the other hand, an average estate running at a loss of, say £8000 a year (see Egdell, 1995), may be a quite acceptable sum to pay for a holiday in which much pleasure is given to the owner, his family and their guests.

[3] As numbers increase, the herd becomes more productive in terms of the potential numbers of beasts that can be taken, but the stress imposed on individuals means that they become less productive: the hinds become less fertile and produce lighter calves; mortality increases. The stags, similarly, do not grow so big and have less imposing antlers.

[4] It is still a commonly held misconception that quality of antler is inherited. It is clear that size of antlers in red deer is for the most part derived from quality of habitat.

[5] Models should be treated with caution as they can be misleading, if they are misapplied. A recent example of a case where a model went badly wrong is that of the Grand Banks fisheries (*New Scientist,* 16 September 1995).

[6] There is a surprising interest to date and a video and booklet about crofter forestry have been circulating (R Dunsmore, personal communication).

[7] Grants have been paid on similar areas of regeneration in the two previous years (R Dunsmore, personal communication).

[8] In 1993, the question was raised as to whether Creag Meagaidh NNR, if it were privately owned, would be eligible under WGS2 for grant aid under the regeneration option. Discussions were held with the Forestry Authority and a desk study undertaken. The area of the reserve considered suitable for a hypothetical application under

WGS2 amounted to 600 hectares. According to the rates of grant then available, this could have resulted in the theoretical payment of a very substantial sum. When WGS3 replaced WGS2, Tilhill Economic Forestry was commissioned to carry out the study outlined in the main text. There is a rule that one government body may not give grants to another and that is why the application for WGS2 and 3 could never be more than hypothetical.

L. GILL

Fresh water and
woodland – a
waterfall in the Coille
Coire Chrannaig.

CHAPTER V: CREAG MEAGAIDH — THE FUTURE

Creag Meagaidh means different things to different people. To the owners and factors of the neighbouring estates it is a nature reserve and so has different objectives from theirs: the management of plantation forestry, sheep farming, deer forest and grouse moor. For some nature conservationists it is a designated area (SSSI and NNR, SPA and SAC), a refuge for the mountain ringlet butterfly, an important site for *Racomitrium* heath, dotterel, montane scrub willow and regenerating birchwood. For another kind of conservationist it is all of these things, but it is also an example of how the wider landscape of the Highlands might develop: what has happened at Creag Meagaidh in the last ten years is a sign of things to come.

Monadhliath has a heavy density of red deer and there is pressure for this to be reduced. The estates fear a future in which there are fewer red deer and the viability of their deer stalking enterprises is put in jeopardy. Perhaps the problems that have resulted in part from past failure to co-operate will lead to the involvement of deer management groups in more co-operative management, leading to sustainable resolutions? To the outsider looking in it seems odd that red deer as *ferae naturae*, belonging to no-one until they are shot or caught, should often be treated so much as domestic stock, only to be shot somewhere else. Co-operative management is a necessity and, as Allan Gordon Cameron

asked early this century, a part of this will include the cessation, eventually, of the absurdity of feeding supposedly wild deer in winter (Cameron, 1923).

Sheep farming has a history of economic difficulty and the future is unlikely to be different. The short-term future is likely to be one in which some agri-environment measures will offer a modicum of support to supplement reduced headage payments for the ewes kept by the farmer. Many sheep farmers will continue to try to spread their capital costs by taking on more land without employing more labour or buying more machinery.[1] There may be increased interest in breeding sheep that have 'easy care' characteristics, following the New Zealand model. In situations where farmers have relatively large areas of inbye land, they may remove their sheep from the hills and intensify on the lower ground. This may leave ground at middle altitudes available for forestry. Where farmers have grazing above the tree line there may even be a return to a form of transhumance, whereby sheep that winter and are lambed inbye are put up to the hill grazings beyond the tree line for the summer before returning to the lower grazings in the autumn. If land is not available for expansion, sheep farmers may seek to reduce costs in other ways. For example, they may reduce expenditure on maintenance of their property, or lay off shepherds and make more use of contract labour at the busiest times of the year (S Ashworth, personal communication). These are speculations for the future. In the longer term, prices for sheep meat and wool are likely to depend on those obtainable on the world market. The presumption is that prices will fall and that hill sheep farming will become even more difficult, making farmers more dependent on support measures, or providing more opportunities for forest regeneration, but who knows?

The recent history of forestry in this country has included ownership by private landowners, forestry companies and the Forestry Commission. The desire of government to privatise publicly owned assets has given new opportunities to forestry companies, but the United Kingdom's support for rural development forestry in the third world has led to groups in this country asking why rural communities here should not own and manage land themselves. The campaign for community forestry has been given further support by the British government's commitment to the Rio Convention (1992) and the Helsinki Agreement (1993). These two important agreements helped consolidate a new place for social values and local interests in national forestry policy (Callander, 1995). The Rio principles and the Helsinki guidelines have become the basis of forestry policy, as spelt out in *Sustainable Forestry – the U K Programme* (HMSO, 1994). Both start from the commitment that: *'Forest resources and forest lands should be sustainably managed to meet the social, economic, ecological, cultural and spiritual needs of present and future generation.'*

The Helsinki guidelines go further to define sustainable management as: *'The stewardship and use of forests and forest lands in a way, and at a rate, that maintains their biodiversity, productivity, regeneration capacity, vitality and their potential to fulfil, now and in the future, the relevant ecological, economic and social functions, at local, national and global levels and that does not cause damage to other ecosystems.'* The acceptance of these important principles and the success of the idea of the Millennium Forest augur well for a future for the new forestry, and so for new values for the land and its use.

These possibilities, if they are realised to any great extent and tied in with the future for sheep farming outlined above, may bring about a different landscape from the one that we have at present through so much of the Highlands. We may imagine a situation in which the wooded landscapes of Strathspey and Deeside are expanded to cover much more of the region.[2] This would be a countryside in which a range of types of ownership with their variety of land uses might co-exist, but in which sustainable forestry using native species would become prominent. Management groups, similar in concept to deer management groups, would discuss woodland management, as is being done in embryonic form in Deeside (R

Callander, personal communication), and perhaps market their produce co-operatively.

What of Creag Meagaidh in this landscape? In the past few years, the upgrading of the A86 has altered the line of the road at Moy, and the associated fencing has been beneficial to the reserve in that it has contributed to the control of the movement of sheep onto it. However, the proposed line of the future upgraded road, although less damaging than might have been the case, is bound to have some adverse impact on the slopes of Am Meall and its regenerating woodland. Apart from this, however, the National Nature Reserve will continue as a landmark of innovation: the deer will be managed, as they are at present, to allow natural regeneration to happen and forest to evolve as part of a deer management policy agreed with the neighbouring estates in the Monadhliath. In terms of the woodland, the embryo of the future may already lie within the reserve – a few young native pine saplings are growing there, and oak exists on the slopes of Am Meall, as do representatives of several other native species (Fry, 1990). The simple future would be a process of succession to pine and oak woodland among the birch, particularly at lower levels, with a predominantly birch forest at higher altitudes up to the tree line. Perhaps the pine will penetrate among the birch as it advances up towards the head of Coire Ardair. In this landscape of mixed woodland, heath and montane heath, there will be heavier, larger deer (stags with bigger antlers). Hinds will be more fertile (Clutton-Brock and Albon,

1989). There will be red grouse and the likelihood of a greater abundance than there has been for some time of black grouse. Leaf fall from the trees will enrich the waters of the burns and lochs and feed invertebrates. These, in turn, will feed trout, charr and the young of the salmon. As leaf fall from the growing forest increases, so will the potential productivity of the freshwater ecosystem.

Walkers and climbers will continue to visit the NNR on their way up the hills and to the cliffs, and they will admire the growing and spreading woods and the flowering herb layer. All this is foreseen in the context of the changing landscape, described earlier, and that context may itself be necessary for Creag Meagaidh to survive, for it is clear that birchwoods are mobile and need room:

'Woodlands commonly show regeneration cycles. These spatial fluctuations in composition are particularly marked in the boreal zone, which includes the Scottish Highlands, where birch, pine and perhaps even oak woods effectively move about with time during natural regeneration cycles and succession. Given this, and also the dynamic nature of many moorland vegetation mosaics, it is clear that upland nature reserves need to be large if there is to be any chance of maintaining vegetation diversity through natural or semi-natural processes. Individual reserves should preferably be in thousands of hectares, and certainly in hundreds, rather than in just tens of hectares' (Miles, 1988).

L. GILL

The land revives.

schoolchildren. It will go on showing people that regeneration of hill land is possible.

In this future we see a landscape in which there are diversity, sustainability and biological productivity; a landscape in which the desire of the Association of Deer Management Groups for open landscape can be reconciled to a considerable extent with the desire of the community foresters for their forested landscape; a landscape in which the needs of the catchment manager and fisheries' interests coincide increasingly with those of the sheep farmer. If this is the future, the experience at Creag Meagaidh will have played an important part in its achievement. Let us see what the years will bring.

Perhaps, some bold souls, when the time comes right, will reintroduce wolves, wild boar, lynx and beaver. If this happens, and the land can hold these former natives of these islands, then the world will be very different.

Creag Meagaidh has been a beacon and a starting point, but the reserve will have to live in a matrix of sustainable forest and hill if it is not to suffer the fate of an island. This weakness is also its urgency. At the beginning of this book, it was stated that SNH had undertaken the project of woodland regeneration at Creag Meagaidh and saw that what had happened might be interesting to the wider world. In this guise of demonstration site the NNR will go on drawing visitors, whether landowners, land managers or

[1] This is unlikely on the deer range, but there is some overlap between sheep ground and deer forest.

[2] I take the region to include the whole upland area north of the Great Highland Boundary Fault, and to include islands.

BIBLIOGRAPHY

Aitken R (198–) Scottish Mountain Footpaths. CCS, Perth.

Aldhous J R (ed.) (1995) Our Pinewood Heritage. Forestry Commission, Edinburgh.

Armstrong A M and Mather A S (1983) Landownership and land use in the Scottish Highlands. O'Dell Memorial Monograph, Dept. of Geography, University of Aberdeen.

Baines D and Hudson P J (1995) The decline of black grouse in Scotland and northern England. Bird Study, Vol. 42, pp. 122–131.

Balharry R and Thompson D B A (1991) Deer management: shared responsibility and heritage stewardship. Paper to the Cairngorms Working Group.

Barrow G W S (1981) Kingship and Unity. Edinburgh University Press, Edinburgh.

Begon M, Harper J L and Townsend C R (1990) Ecology – Individuals, Populations and Communities. Blackwell Scientific Publications, Oxford.

Birks H H, Birks J H B, Kaland P E and Moe D (1988) The Cultural Landscape, Past, Present and Future. Cambridge University Press, Cambridge.

Breadalbane, Marchioness of (1907) High Tops of the Black Mount. Wm. Blackwood & Sons, Edinburgh.

Brown A F and Bainbridge I P (1995) Grouse moors and upland breeding birds. In: **Thompson D B A, Hester A J and Usher M B** (1995)Heaths and Moorland – Cultural Landscapes. HMSO.

Buckland S T, Ahmadi S, Staines B W, Gordon I J and Youngson R W (1996) Estimating the minimum population size that allows a given annual number of mature red deer stags to be culled sustainably. Journal of Applied Ecology, Vol. 33, pp. 118–130.

Bumsted J M (1982) The People's Clearance: Highland Emigration to British North America: 1770–1815. Edinburgh University Press, Edinburgh.

Callander R (1995) Forests and People in Rural Scotland. Rural Forum Scotland, Perth.

Cameron A G (1923) The Wild Red Deer of Scotland. Blackwood and Sons, Edinburgh.

Close-Brooks J (1986) Exploring Scotland's Heritage – The Highlands. HMSO, Edinburgh.

Clutton-Brock T H and Albon S D (1989) Red Deer in the Scottish Highlands. BSP Professional Books, Oxford.

Clutton-Brock T H and Lonergan M E (1994) Culling regimes and sex ratio biases in Highland red deer. Journal of Applied Ecology, Vol. 31, pp. 521–527.

Darling F Fraser (1937) A Herd of Red Deer: A Study in Animal Behaviour. Oxford University Press, London.

Darling F Fraser (1955) West Highland Survey: An Essay in Human Ecology. Oxford University Press, Oxford.

Darling F Fraser (1969) Wilderness and Plenty – The Reith Lectures for 1969.

Dwelly E (1949) The Illustrated Gaelic – English Dictionary, 5th edn. Alex MacLaren and Sons, Glasgow.

Egdell J M (1995) The Economics of Upland Grouse Shooting: Implications for Wildlife. RSPB, Edinburgh.

Donaldson J C and Brown H M (eds) (1984) Munro's Tables. Scottish Mountaineering Trust.

Ferguson A (1995) Report on Electrofishing of Loch Laggan Tributaries – Creag Meagaidh NNR. Unpublished typescript, SNH, Achantoul.

Francis J M, Balharry R and Thompson D B A (1990) The implications for upland management. In: **Rose H** (ed.) Deer, Mountains and Man. RDC/BDS, Inverness.

Fraser-Mackintosh C (1890) <u>Letters of Two Centuries.</u> Inverness.

Fraser-Mackintosh C (1897) <u>Antiquarian Notes</u> (second series), Vol. 131, pp. 364–365.

Fry G (1990) <u>Creag Meagaidh National Nature Reserve: A Woodland Survey.</u> Unpublished report, SNH, Achantoul.

Gilbert J M (1979) <u>Hunting and Hunting Reserves in Medieval Scotland.</u> John Donald, Edinburgh.

Gilvear D, Hanley N, Maitland P and Peterken G (1995) <u>Wild Rivers. Phase 1: Technical Paper.</u> A Report to WWF Scotland, Stirling.

Gimingham C (1995) Heaths and moorland: an overview of ecological change. In: **Thompson D B A, Hester A J and Usher M B** <u>Heaths and Moorland – Cultural Landscapes.</u> HMSO, London.

Goldsmith F B (1993) Monitoring for conservation. In: **Goldsmith F B and Warren A** (eds) <u>Conservation in Progress.</u> John Wiley & Sons, Chichester.

Gordon G (1995) A speech to the Standing Conference on Countryside Sports, delivered on the 26 October 1995 at Battleby, Perth.

Grant of Laggan A (1845) <u>Letters from the Mountains.</u> Longman, London.

Grant I F (1961) <u>Highland Folkways.</u> Routledge and Kegan Paul, London.

Grant I F (1980) <u>Along a Highland Road.</u> Shepheard-Walwyn, London.

Grant I F and Cheape (1987) <u>Periods in Highland History.</u> Shepheard Walwyn, London.

Gray M (1957) <u>The Highland Economy 1750–1850.</u> Edinburgh.

Halcrow V (1994) <u>Creag Meagaidh NNR: Site Management Brief.</u> Internal report, SNH.

Haldane A R B (1962) <u>New Ways through the Glens.</u> Nelson, Edinburgh and London.

Hansard Vol 493 10 Feb 1988. A question in the House of Lords by Lord Burton on the expense of extracting stags by helicopter from Creag Meagaidh NNR.

Hart-Davies D (1978) <u>Monarchs of the Glen: A History of Deer-Stalking in the Scottish Highlands.</u> Cape, London.

Hester A (1995) <u>Scrub in the Scottish Uplands.</u> SNH Review no. 24, Edinburgh.

Hester A and Sydes C (forthcoming) In: **Stevenson A C and Thompson D B A** (eds) (1993) Long-term changes in the extent of heather moorland in upland Britain and Ireland: palaeological evidence for the importance of grazing. <u>The Holocene,</u> 3 (1), 7–76.

Hester A J, Miles J and Gimingham C H (1991a) Succession from heather moorland to birch woodland. I. Experimental alteration of specific environmental conditions in the field. <u>Journal of Ecology,</u> 79, 303–315.

Hester A J, Miles J and Gimingham C H (1991b) Succession from heather moorland to birch woodland. III. Seed availability, germination and early growth. <u>Journal of Ecology,</u> Vol. 79, pp. 329–344.

HMSO (1972) <u>Forestry in Great Britain – An Inter-Departmental Cost/Benefit Analysis.</u> National Audit Office.

HMSO (1994) <u>Sustainable Forestry – The UK Programme.</u>

Holloway (1967) The effects of red deer and other animals on naturally regenerated Scots pine. PhD thesis. University of Aberdeen, quoted in SNH Policy Paper, <u>Red Deer and the Natural Heritage</u> (1994).

Hunter J (1994) <u>A Dance Called America: The Scottish Highlands, the United States and Canada.</u> Mainstream, Edinburgh.

Hunter J (1995) On the Other Side of Sorrow. Mainstream, Edinburgh.

Jarvie E (1980) The Red Deer Industry: Finance and Employment 1978/79. SLF, Edinburgh.

Lister-Kaye Sir J (1994) Ill Fares the Land. Barail, Sleat.

Lovelock J (1990) The Ages of Gaia. Oxford University Press, Oxford.

Macfarlane W (1908) Geographical Collections relating to Scotland. Sir A Mitchell and JT Clark (eds). Scottish History Society, Edinburgh.

McGilvray J and Perman R (1991) Grouse Shooting in Scotland: an analysis of its importance to the economy and environment. University of Strathclyde. Report to the Game Conservancy Trust.

MacKenzie A (1883) The History of the Highland Clearances. Inverness.

MacLeod A (1952) Orain Dhonnchaidh Bhain. The Scottish Academic Press, Edinburgh.

Macpherson A (1893) Glimpses of Church and Social Life in the Highlands in Olden Times. Blackwoods, Edinburgh.

McVean D N and Lockie J D (1969) Ecology and Land Use in Upland Scotland. Edinburgh University Press, Edinburgh.

McVean D N and Ratcliffe D A (1962) Plant Communities of the Scottish Highlands: A Study of Scottish Mountain, Moorland and Forest Vegetation. HMSO, London.

Maitland P S and Campbell R N (1992) Freshwater Fishes. HarperCollins, London and Glasgow.

Marshall W (1794) General View of the Agriculture of the Central Highlands, London.

Marx K (1976) Collected works, Moscow, quoted in Richards E (1985) History of the Highland Clearances, Volume 2. Croom Helm, London.

Mather A S (1992) Land use, physical sustainability and conservation in Highland Scotland. Land Use Policy, pp. 99–110.

Miles J (1985) The pedogenic effects of different species and vegetation types and the implications of succession. Journal of Soil Science, 36, 571–584.

Miles J (1988) Vegetation and soil change in the uplands. In: **Usher and Thompson** (eds) Ecological Change in the Uplands. Blackwell Scientific Publications, Oxford.

Mollison D (ed.) (1992) Wilderness with People: The Management of Wild Land. JMT, Musselburgh.

Moore N W (1987) The Bird of Time. Cambridge University Press, Cambridge.

Moore S E A (1994) Creag Meagaidh – A Review of Past Management 1985–1993. Unpublished report, SNH, Achantoul.

National Audit Office (1986) Review of Forestry Commission's Objectives and Achievements. HMSO.

Nature Conservancy Council (1987) A Management Plan for Creag Meagaidh NNR. NCC, Achantoul.

Nautilus Consultants (1995) In association with Smiths Gore. An economic Assessment of the major Land Uses in the Scottish Uplands. A Report for Scottish Natural Heritage. Edinburgh.

Nethersole-Thompson D and Watson A (1981) The Cairngorms. Melvens, Perth.

O'Donovan R (1988) Creag Meagaidh National Nature Reserve: an Historical Land Use Survey. SNH, Achantoul.

Patterson G (1993) The Value of Birch in Upland Forests for Wildlife Conservation. FC Bulletin 109. Forestry Commission, Alice Holt, Farnham.

Pearson of Rannoch, Lord (1995) A speech to the conference held jointly by the Royal Society for the Protection of Birds and the British Deer Society at Eden Court Theatre, Inverness, October 1995.

Peterken G (1993) Woodland Conservation and Management, 2nd edn. Chapman & Hall, London.

Phillips J and Watson A (1995) In: **Thompson D B A, Hester A J and Usher M B** (1995) Heaths and Moorland: Cultural Landscapes. HMSO, London.

Ratcliffe D A (1977) A Nature Conservation Review. Cambridge University Press, Cambridge.

Rawson (1990) A window on Meagaidh. Great Outdoors, February, pp. 45–47.

Red Deer Commission Annual Reports. RDC, Inverness.

Report of the Commission of Inquiry into the Condition of the Crofters and Cottars of the Highlands and Islands of Scotland (1884) 'The Napier Report'.

Richards E (1982) A History of the Highland Clearances. Croom Helm, London.

Richardson S, Walker A and Clothier R (1994) Ben Nevis, Rock and Ice Climbs. SMC, Edinburgh.

Robertson J (1808) General View of the Agriculture in the County of Inverness.

Scottish Natural Heritage (1994) Red Deer and the Natural Heritage. SNH Policy Paper, Edinburgh.

Scottish Natural Heritage (1995) Management Plan for Creag Meagaidh January 1995–December 1999. SNH, Achantoul.

Scrope W (1838) The Art of Deer Stalking. John Murray, London.

Sheddon C B (1992) Red Deer in Scotland. A report by the British Association for Shooting and Conservation, Dunkeld.

Sinton Revd Dr T (1906) The Poetry of Badenoch. The Northern Counties Printing and Publishing Company, Inverness.

Sinton T (1910) By Loch and River. The Northern Counties Printing and Publishing Company, Inverness.

Smout T C (1993) Scotland since Prehistory. Scottish Cultural Press, Aberdeen.

Staines B W and Balharry R (1994). Red Deer and their Management in the Cairngorms. A report to the Cairngorms Working Party, Achantoul.

Staines B W and Scott D (1992) Recreation and Red Deer: a Preliminary Review of the Issues. ITE, Banchory

Stevenson A C and Thompson D B A (1993) Long-term changes in the extent of heather moorland in upland Britain and Ireland: palaeological evidence for the importance of grazing. The Holocene, 3, 70–76.

Sydes C and Miller G R (1988) Range management and nature conservation in the British uplands. In: **Usher M B and Thompson D B A** (eds) Ecological Change in the Uplands.

Tait J H (1928) The Game and Fishing Laws of Scotland. 2nd edn. W. Green and Son, Edinburgh.

Thompson D B A and Miles J (1995) Heaths and moorland: some conclusions and questions about environmental change. In: **Thompson D B A, Hester A J and Usher M B** (eds) Heaths and Moorland: Cultural Landscapes. HMSO, London.

Thompson D B A and Whitfield D P (1993) Research progress report. Scottish Birds, Vol. 17, pp. 1–8.

Thompson D B A, Galbraith H and Horsfield D (1987) Ecology and resources of Britain's mountain plateaux: land use conflicts and impacts. In: **Bell M and Bunce R G H** Agriculture and Conservation in the Hills and Uplands. ITE Symposium no. 23.

Thompson D B A, Hester A J and Usher M B (1995) Heaths and Moorland: Cultural Landscapes. HMSO, London.

Tomkins S C (1986) The Theft of the Hills. The Ramblers' Association, London.

Usher M B and Thompson D B A (eds) (1988) Ecological Change in the Uplands. Blackwell Scientific Publications, Oxford.

Veblen T (1899) The Theory of the Leisure Class. Penguin (1994).

Watson A and Allan E (1990) Depopulation by clearances and non-enforced emigration in the North-East of Scotland. Northern Scotland, Vol. 10, pp. 31–46.

Watson W J (1926) The History of the Celtic Place Names of Scotland. Republished in 1993 by Birlinn Ltd, Edinburgh.

Watson W J (1959) Bardachd Gaidhlig, 3rd edn. A Learmonth & Son, Stirling.

Whyte I (1979) Agriculture and Society in Seventeenth Century Scotland. John Donald, Edinburgh.

Youngson A J (1973) After the '45. Edinburgh University Press, Edinburgh.

APPENDIX A

Place names on the Creag Meagaidh National Nature Reserve, Laggan, Badenoch by Ian A Fraser, The School of Scottish Studies, Edinburgh University

A guide to approximate pronunciation of the names is found after the translation in square brackets.

A'Bhuidheanach – the yellow one, or the yellow place [ivuienach]

A'Choille Mhór – the big forest [ichullyivor]

Aberarder – confluence of the high water (see Watson (1926) p. 454)

Aiste Mhór – possibly a misspelling of ciste 'coffin' or 'chest', a term occasionally found in rocky hill names

Allt a'Choire Chomharsain – burn of the sideways corrie. Dwelly (1949) gives, for **comhair** 'direction or tendency, forward, backward, sideways, etc.' (see Watson (1926) p. 237). Words in **comh** always signify 'together'

Allt Coire Ardair – burn of the high water corrie [alt'korardir]

Allt Dubh – black burn

Allt na Creige Tarsuinn – burn of the cross rock [altnikrekitarsin]

Allt nan Cearcall – burn of the circles [altninkerkil]

Am Meall – the hill [immjall]

An Cearcallach – the circle place [inkerkilach]

An Geurachadh – the sharp place [ingayrachik]

An Sidhean – the fairy hill [insheeun]

Bealach a'Geurachaidh – pass of the sharp place [bjalachugayrachik]

Bealach a'Ghoire – pass of the crowing [bjalachughuru] – ('u' as in m<u>u</u>st)

Binnein shuas – the upper pinnacle [binyinhoous]

Carn liath – hoary cairn [karnleeuh]

Coille a'Choire – wood of the corrie [cullyyuchoru]

Coille Chrannaig – wood of the pulpit [cullychranek]

Coille Coire Chrannaig – wood of the corrie of the pulpit [cully korichranek]

Coire a'Chriochairein – probably corrie or the boundary place. It is near the boundary, so it may well contain **crioch** 'boundary', 'march', but if so, it is a very unusual ending. It could, however, be **crochaire** 'hangman' from **croch** to 'hang'. If it is a hanging corrie, and it could be just from looking at the map, then there may have been transposition of the 'io'

Coire Choille Rais – corrie of the wooded point [korichullyrash] (see Watson (1926) p. 497–498)

Coire Garbh – rough corrie [korigariv]

Coire nan Gall – corrie of the foreigners, lowlanders or strangers [koriningawl]

Creag Beag – little rock [krekbeck]

Creag Meagaidh – rock of the boggy place [krekmeggy] (see Watson (1926) p. 374–375)

Creag Mhór – big rock [krekvor]

Dail na Mine – haugh of the meal (oatmeal) [dalnimeenu]

Doire nan Dearcag – thicket of the berries [durinindjerkuk]

Drochaid Aberarder – Aberarder Bridge [drochitsh...]

Eilean an Righ – island of the king [elununree]

Glen Shira – glen of the lasting river (see Watson (1926) p. 477)

Innis na Galla – meadow of the bitch (deerhound?) [inishnigallu]

Laggan – little hollow [lagun or lakun]

Lochain na Cailliche – little loch of the old woman [lochunnukalijichu]

Meall an t-snaim – hill of the knot [melintnaim] (not the bird, of course)

Meall Damh – hill of the stags [mjeldaff]

Moy – flat plain

Na Cnapan – the lumps [ni'knahpin]

Poite Coire Ardair – the pot of Coire Ardair [potju]

Puist Coire Ardair – the posts of Coire Ardair [poosht]

Rubha na Magach – point of the frogs, but this is usually the word for a frog or toad, if the first vowel is stressed. If there is no stress, **magach** means 'mocking', 'given to derision' (Dwelly, (1949) p. 622). There may be some historical tradition connected with this promontory, so if there are any natives still around this area, they may know. Also, Ian Fraser would have expected a plural if toads were involved, giving **Rubha nam Magach**, but these are often corrupted

Slugan Coire nan Gall – gorge of the corrie of the foreigners (see Dwelly, (1949) p. 856)

Sròn a'Ghoire – promontory of the crowing or crying [sronughuru]

Tom Bàn – fair or white hillock

Tullochcrom – bent hillock

Uinneag Choire a'Chaorainn – the window of the rowan tree corrie [inyak chori I chiring]

Uinneag Mín Choire – the window of the smooth corrie [inyak meen chori]

APPENDIX B

Red deer monitoring by Peter Reynolds

Table 1: Parameters of a living red deer population, which it is essential to quantify for the purposes of informing objective management decisions

Parameter	How?	When?	Why?
Deer numbers	Ground or helicopter counts	Late winter/early spring when animals concentrated in wintering area	Essential for setting the cull, monitoring the numerical response and evaluating effects on habitats
Population structure	Differentiate stags, hinds and calves during ground or helicopter counts	Late winter/early spring when animals concentrated in wintering area	Essential for setting the cull and monitoring the demographic effects
Recruitment rate	Assess number of surviving calves following winter/early spring mortality from ground or helicopter counts	Late winter/early spring when animals concentrated in wintering area and following period of maximum calf mortality. April probably best month	Prerequisite for setting cull

Table 2: Parameters of culled deer, which it is essential to quantify for the purposes of informing objective management decisions

Parameter	How?	When?	Why?
Category of animal (stag, hind, calf), sex in last case	Self-explanatory	In the larder, or if animals are left on the hill, immediately after culling	These categories provide an essential framework without which age and performance data cannot be meaningfully analysed. They are also fundamental to the understanding of past and future changes in population structure and numbers
Carcass weight	Two options: **Larder carcass weight:** weight of complete animal, less bleedable blood and complete alimentary tract. **Dressed carcass weight with skin:** larder carcass weightless head, feet, heart, liver, lungs, kidneys and fat, udder and genitals	In the larder	When related to age and sex, carcass weight can provide a useful measure of herd condition. Increasing or declining average weights may, for example, be indicative of improving or deteriorating range conditions respectively. For carcass conversion factors see Appendix
Age	Remove lower jaw, label indelibly or tag (cross-referenced to carcass), thoroughly clean jaw and check teeth and then determine age by assessing	Can be done at any stage following cull providing that jaws are labelled and cross-referenced to carcass	Essential information pivotal to the interpretation of weight, condition, reproductive and other demographic parameters. For example, an increasing or decreasing proportion of pregnant one and two-year-olds is a

	stage of tooth eruption and wear.[1,2] Alternatively, age can be determined by sectioning and counting the annual rings in the dental cementum of the lower first molar.[3] If this latter technique is used, jaws should not be boiled, as it can make counting of annual rings difficult		likely response to improving or deteriorating range quality respectively. Also enables cohort analysis to be undertaken such that minimum populations can be determined retrospectively (see Table 3)
Fertility	Remove reproductive tract from all females (uterus, oviduct, ovaries). Cut open uterus. In most females shot during open season, pregnancy indicated by presence of embryo. If large enough, note the sex. Embryos may not be visible in very early stages of pregnancy (before mid-November). In these cases, pregnancy is detected by slicing both ovaries in half. Presence of yellowish gland (corpus luteum), which only persists following fertilisation, is indicative of pregnancy. Record corpora lutea, even if embryos found. For each ovary, note as 1, corpus luteum; 2, corpora lutea or none.[1]	Post mortem in larder	When related to age, fertility provides an essential measure of potential reproductive performance, which is sensitive, especially in one and two-year-olds, to changes in range quality. Also provides supplementary information of value in the interpretation of calf mortality and recruitment rates
Milk or yeld	Examine udder for the presence of milk by squeezing nipple or slicing through the gland. This may not be reliable late January/February, in which case degree of hair cover on udder may help, sparse cover being indicative of milk hinds	Post mortem in larder	The proportion of milk hinds pregnant in the population provides a useful indirect measure of range quality, declining with increased population by density and, thus, increased competition for resources
Condition	**Subjective method:** 'Good', carcass with good covering of fat on the rump and above rib-cage and muscle on saddle convex or straight line 'Average', carcass with little or no fat cover, ribs beginning to show through flank and saddle muscle forming a straight line 'Poor', carcass with no fat cover, ribs clearly visible and saddle muscle concave	Post mortem in larder	Condition scores, in combination with age data, will provide a useful indirect measure of range quality. For example, antler size and weight are strongly influenced by environmental factors. At the very least, the subjective assessment of carcass condition should be used, together with antler weight

Objective methods:		
Kidney fat index (weight of perinephric fat plus kidneys divided by kidney weight)[4]		
Antler weight		

Table 3: Parameters of living deer populations, which could usefully be collected, but not essential

Parameter	How?	When?	Why?
Adult natural mortality	In average years, adult (one or more years old) mortality rates can be assumed to be in the region of 2–3%. Following wet winters and/or late springs, surveys should be undertaken to record all natural deaths of adult animals (location, sex and age)	Early spring, following peak period of mortality during the winter months	In setting annual culls, losses due to natural mortality (the bulk of which tends to occur after culling) should be taken into account
Calving rate	Record calf/hind ratio in summer	July/August when most calves are conspicuous	Comparison of calving and recruitment rates will provide a useful measure of calf mortality during the summer to winter period
Minimum population size	Cohort analysis: record the age and sex of each animal culled[1]	Annual: requires data collected over several years	Provides an accurate retrospective check on minimum population size[1]
Summer range use	Map the distribution and numbers of deer on as many occasions as possible during the summer	Summer months, say May – September	Quantifies and defines the summer range of deer and provides a focus for the monitoring of range condition
Indirect measures of range use and deer density	Dung group counts, together with measures of defaecation rates and decay rates[1]	Any time, but spring counts are easier before vegetation growth obscures dung groups	Provides an estimate of the average deer density over a period of several months in specific habitats. Can be a useful complement to counts of animals, which represent a single instant in time[1]
Antler cleaning date	Assess proportion of stags that have begun cleaning their antlers by a particular date. Differentiate between mature (aged five years and over) and immature (less than five years or older) animals. This is important since immature stags tend to clean later than mature stags	Determine proportion of stags that have begun cleaning during the last ten days in August. Precise period not critical as long as it is consistent between years	Antler cleaning is dependent upon a rise in testosterone levels, the timing of which is influenced by condition. Changes in the proportion of animals cleaning by a particular date therefore provides an index of changes in animal condition
Antler casting date	Assess proportion of stags that have cast their antlers by a particular date. Differentiate between mature (aged five years and over) and immature (less than five years but yearlings or older) animals	Determine proportion of stags that have cast their antlers by the end of the first week in April	The timing of antler casting is influenced by condition. Changes in the proportion of animals casting by a particular date may therefore provide an index of animal condition

APPENDIX

Carcass conversion factors (%) for red deer in autumn (from Mitchell and Crisp 1981)[5]

Class of animal	Live animal (%)	Larder carcass (complete animal less blood and alimentary tract,%)	Dressed carcass weight with skin (larder carcass weight less head, feet, heart, liver, lungs, kidneys, fat, udder and genitals,%)
Stags (full grown)	100	73	56
Hinds (adult yeld)	100	66	52
Hinds (milk)	100	60	45
Calves	100	67	53

[1] Ratcliffe P R (1987) The Management of Red Deer in Upland Forests. Forestry Commission Bulletin no. 71.

[2] Red Deer Commission (1981) Red Deer Management. HMSO.

[3] Ratcliffe P R and Mayle B A (1992) Roe Deer Biology and Management. Forestry Commission Bulletin no. 105.

[4] Mitchell B, McCowan D and Nicholson I A (1976) Annual cycles of body weight and condition in Scottish red deer. Journal of Zoology, Vol. 180, pp. 107–127.

[5] Mitchell B and Crisp J M (1981) Some properties of red deer at exceptionally high population density in Scotland. Journal of Zoology, Vol. 193, pp. 157–169.

APPENDIX C

Research/survey/monitoring projects
(listed by topic)

GEOLOGY/GEOMORPHOLOGY

Earth Science Documentation Series (SNH Earth Science Branch)
Creag Meagaidh SSSI, Sarah Keast, December 1993. A useful plain English summary of features and their management requirements. Contains other references [Achantoul library].

HISTORY/LAND USE

An Historical Land Use Survey (Creag Meagaidh NNR), Roger O'Donovan 1988.
Field survey of historical artifacts, 53 recorded on a map; search of historical records; interviews with local people.
Aerial photograph coverage, note and map [Scientific file I].
Evaluation of effectiveness of aerial photographs (helicopter) to monitor path erosion and tree regeneration, Karen Johnson (1992) [Achantoul library S24 and Scientific file 3].
Could be used to monitor changes in landscape for NVC survey or for interpretation. Vegetation and regeneration monitoring requires low, accurate flying over precise flight paths.
Periglacial features map/file note Chattopadhyay, 1981 [Scientific file I].
Rainfall map [Scientific file].

FLORA

VEGETATION

Upland Survey Project: Site Report 1982. Horsfield D and Sydes C.
Vegetation Survey Moy Estate. Report to Fountain Forestry. Birse E L (1983).
Vegetation Survey. Ratcliffe D (1957). BRC record cards, stand-type map, sample plot descriptions.

WOODLANDS

Woodland Record Card: Ground Flora Plots. Keith Kirby (1983)
Birchwoods – Study of Distribution, Density, Regeneration Campbell D (1985) [Achantoul library, report C28].

Deer Transect Monitoring – Summary Clark P.
Tree Survey of Coire Ardair Anon (1990).
Regeneration in Am Meall Exclosure Clark P (1991). The number of trees on transects in Am Meall increasing.
Survey of Wood below Main Road at Aberarder Anon (1991).
Aberarder Alder Wood Survey Clark P (1991).
Distribution of Trees And Seedlings Allemand M (1985) (foreign exchange student) [Creag Meagaidh box file].
A Woodland Survey Fry G (1990). Map areas of established woodland, areas of regeneration, set up permanent quadrats in regenerating areas.
The Am Meall Deer Fence: A Report on its Future Carr T (1992). Ten transects 30 m wide.

BOTANY

RBG Edinburgh Survey (1981) [Scientific file I].
Update, June 1989 [Scientific file II].
Plant Records McCallum Webster M (1984) [Scientific file I].
Lucy Rankin (1984) [Scientific file I].
BSBI Cards Murray C W via Barron M [Scientific file II].
Species List Gilbert D (September 1987) [Scientific file II].
Updated to include 200 species (February 1990) [Scientific file II].
Juniper: Map showing Occurrence of Juniper spp. [Scientific file III].
Willow Identification: Three Alpine Willows (September 1992) [Scientific file III].
Ferns, Horsetails and Clubmosses 17 spp.
Lichen List Fryday A (1990) [Scientific file II].
Bryophyte List Averis B (1986) [Scientific file II].
Fungi List (1993) [Scientific file III].
Flora Master List. All records added, for five-year periods [held at Achantoul].

AQUATIC

Diatom/water chemistry-based assessment of the acidification status of selected NCC sites (Creag Meagaidh: four lochs, three burns).
Fish Survey Lyle A (1988) ITE Edinburgh [Scientific file II].
Investigation of Possible Development of a Gill-net Fishery for Arctic Charr in Loch Laggan Greer R and Collen P (no date) [Creag Meagaidh box file, Achantoul].

FAUNA

Fauna Master List. Records added for periods of five years [held at Achantoul].

INVERTEBRATES

MOLLUSCA

Search for Vertigo modesta, a small snail (Summer 1991) Creag Meagaidh file, Scientific file II).

INSECTA

Altitudinal Succession Horsfield D.
Beetle Fauna/Trapping Owen J A (1987).
Hoverflies (Syrphydae) 52 spp, one RDB, two notables. Levy E T and Levy D A (1989 and 1990) Could be added to [Achantoul, box file].
Moths Clark P (1991) Traps at seven sites on NNR [Scientific file III].
Butterflies: Small Mountain Ringlet Erebia epiphron Report Baines M (1993).

BIRD LIST

May 1985–May 1986, December 1985–August 1986 Keenan S.
Winter Records Duncan K (1990) [Scientific file II].
Records Holloway S (7/1/90–24/1/90).
BTO Record Card Duncan K (9/7/91).

MAMMAL

Records Duncan K (September 1990–December 1990).
Small Mammal Survey Harjuhahto T (1987) [Scientific file II].
Red deer: Coloured collar tagging, ear tagging of calves. Not collated, notes on red deer files only.
Evaluation of Airborne Thermal Imaging for Census of Red Deer Populations in Extensive Open Habitats Reynolds P et al. (March 1993).
Red deer count at Tulloch varied by 6–12% from ground counts. Ground counts at Creag Meagaidh very similar to aerial infrared count. Infrared counts used 50–75% fewer man–hours, but gave less information on population structure.
Effects of Red Deer Browsing on Tree Regeneration at Creag Meagaidh NNR Daniels M (May 1992) Institute of Ecology and Resource Management, University of Edinburgh. Discusses pellet analysis, deer density, seedlings in diet and browsing damage.

HUMAN LAND USE

Skiing Developments, Field Survey Data (1979) [Scientific file I].
Visitor/Footpath Monitoring Methods Riach J W (1986) DRLP Investigation. Path photography, aerial photography, desk study, people counters. Analysis of visitor use in winter.
Damage: Monitoring (photographic) of ATV Damage Rankin L (March 1988) [Archive file, slides in slide cabinet, Achantoul].

APPENDIX D

Creag Meagaidh NNR monitoring projects

Eagle activity

This includes observation of the activities of eagles in spring in relation to possible attempts to breed.

Black grouse leks

Leks are surveyed annually. An increase in numbers of cocks has been observed.

Moth trapping

Regular trapping is carried out throughout the year. The reserve list includes 126 species now. This is not expected to be the final figure. There are new records every year, including two during the winter of 1995/96.

Grass field monitoring

A botanical survey was carried out before a grazing regime was established, according to ESA criteria. The survey was done before the grass park was let for grazing by cattle. Sheep that are gathered on the reserve are put into the park until collection by their owners.

Count captured/culled red deer

This survey includes the data collected on all captured and culled deer.

Small mammals

A baseline survey was carried out in 1987.

Red deer monthly counts

Monthly counts of the red deer are carried out to assess changes in numbers in response to culling.

Sheep counts

These are carried out every month to assess the numbers of sheep marauding on to the NNR.

Monitor golden eagle

This is distinct from the project mentioned above. Eyries are checked every year for breeding success. There has been no success recently.

Dotterel counts

The breeding population is monitored every five years to assess responses to changes in the grazing regime.

Grouse and heather project

A baseline survey was carried out to assess the grouse population on Am Meall and in Coire Ardair. The dominance of heather as a component of the plant community was assessed also. It is planned to follow up this survey every five years.

Common bird census

The population of small birds is monitored every five years using the criteria of the national common bird census, but the information is used internally, because the survey is only carried out every five years rather than every year, as it is for the national survey.

Mountain ringlet transect

A transect is walked every summer to assess the population of Mountain Ringlets and detect any changes in their numbers.

Monitor recovery after ATV use

This project records information on an area where ATVs are used and checks progress in the process of recovery.

Deer/tree regeneration transects

This is the continuing annual survey on seven transects to monitor the number of trees gaining height on the surrounding vegetation (see the section on habitat and regeneration in Chapter III).

Windblow 1989/91

Trees blown over in the gales of 1989 were recorded in March 1989. Sixty-two trees out of 180 trees on the transect were damaged, representing 31% of total woodland damaged. The number of fallen trees was recorded. Gale damage to the alder wood in 1993 was recorded. Levels of damage and root plates exposed.

Am Meall plots

A system of recording tree regeneration within Am Meall has been established and has been recorded again in 1995/96.

Fiona Stewart's work

The effect of browsing on tree establishment has been researched by Fiona Stewart, and plots established. More monitoring is possible.

Kingussie High School tree growth plot

The third year biology class of Kingussie High School have been recording plots within the deer/tree regeneration transects to assess the growth of tree species.

Monitor Racomitrium heath

Baseline monitoring has been carried out on the high plateau heath to record vegetational changes due to reduction in grazing pressure and, primarily, in areas where the sheep numbers have been reduced.

Visitor counts

Counting has been done since 1987 at the car park. In 1992, another electronic counter was installed on the path above Aberarder Farmhouse. Numbers of visitors are counted daily and the figures are collated each month.

Helicopter/regeneration transects

Aerial photographs have been taken of the deer/tree regeneration transects to assess visible changes to the vegetation. The sleeper walkway is monitored at the same time.

APPENDIX E

Code of conduct for the extraction of deer carcasses

Creag Meagaidh National Nature Reserve

The following is a code of conduct for the retrieval of deer carcasses shot on the hill at Creag Meagaidh NNR and the options are in order of preference:

Option 1: Drag the carcass to the nearest point of collection at roadside.

Option 2: Drag the carcass to the nearest point for collection by pony.

Option 3: Drag the carcass to a point below 400 m where it is convenient for collection by Glencoe.

Therefore, should it be impractical to drag the carcass owing to distance involved, ground conditions, etc. the option of the pony should be considered, and should the number of beasts shot be excessive for the pony then the Glencoe should be considered under an altitude of 400 m. If the number of beasts is large enough (about 20), then the option of a helicopter should also be investigated. It is paramount that this code is followed so that damage to the habitat is kept to an absolute minimum.

The Glencoe also has a system for booking its use and also for logging the journeys, so that a record is kept. The application for its use includes a justification and the consideration of alternative methods. See attached application form.

APPLICATION FOR USE OF AN ATV ON CREAG MEAGAIDH NNR

DATE OF APPLICATION................................ DATE REQUIRED.............................

CLIENT NAME..

PURPOSE OF JOURNEY..

....

DESTINATION AND HASL[1]...

ITEMS TRANSPORTED..

ESTIMATED WEIGHT..

JUSTIFICATION

OTHER MEANS OF MOVING MATERIALS..

NUMBER OF PEOPLE...

NECESSITY OF JOURNEY (HASAWA etc.)[2]..

COULD JOURNEY BE CARRIED OUT AT ANY OTHER TIME?....................................

....

ESTIMATE OF DRIVER TIME...

ARE OTHER STAFF NEEDED?...

APPROVAL AREA OFFICER..

AREA MANAGER...

[1] Height above sea level.   [2] Health and Safety at Work Act.

APPENDIX F

Tables and charts

Table 1: Numbers of red deer counted and culled from Creag Meagaidh

Year	SPRING 85	WINTER 86	SPRING 87	SUMMER 88	SPRING 89	90/91	91/92	92/93	93/94	94/95	95/96
							MEAN OF MONTHLY COUNTS				
Deer counted	1000	689	594	755	148	257	183	225	122	102	86
Stags culled	2	10	63	60	43	35	35	25	25	10	14
Hinds and calves culled	50	180	212	159	47	108	44	72	33	35	46
Live capture of hinds and calves	0	25	96	23	119	47	57	69	25	0	0
Total	52	215	371	242	209	190	136	166	83	45	60

Table 2: Deer counts at Creag Meagaidh from 1977 to 1996 – all spring counts (note the gap 1978–1986)

Year	Source	Stags	Hinds	Calves	Undifferentiated	Total
1977	RDC	72	414	140		626
1987	RDC	52	406	136		594
1988	NCC	9	191	60		260
1989	NCC	2	143	3		148
1990	NCC	10			46	56
1991	NCC	0			84	84
1992	SNH	9			61	70
1993	SNH	27	60	32		119
1994	SNH	1	4	2		7
1995	SNH	8	7	3		18
1996	SNH	0	18	6		24

Chart 1

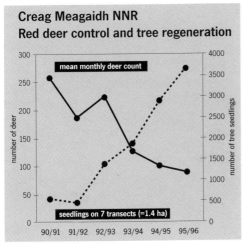

Creag Meagaidh NNR
Red deer control and tree regeneration

Chart 2

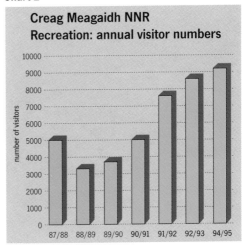

Creag Meagaidh NNR
Recreation: annual visitor numbers

APPENDIX G

Management objectives for Creag Meagaidh NNR according to the Management Plan of 1995

From these aims the following management objectives were proposed:

1. To protect the reserve from influences which might damage the scientific interest.

2. To maintain the diversity of species and habitat and enhance those habitats that appear degraded – in particular, the woodland and scrub elements.

3. To encourage the study of the NNR by continuing to develop a research, survey and monitoring programme.

4. To encourage use of the reserve for education and demonstration purposes and improve interpretation by maintaining links with schools and developing an interpretative plan.

5. To encourage public appreciation of the reserve, subject to objective 1, and to continue with provisions to facilitate an open access policy.

6. To protect as far as possible the present landscape character.

7. To manage the rest of the property outwith the NNR in accordance with good estate management and with a view to achieving other reserve objectives.

   To fulfil other obligations (SNH Management Plan for Creag Meagaidh, 1995).

APPENDIX H

Details of the WGS3 application for Creag Meagaidh NNR

This is a summary of the woodland regeneration scheme that was devised under the auspices of WGS3 by Tilhill Economic Forestry on behalf of SNH. It should be emphasised that it is hypothetical and that the FA considers each case on its merits. Moreover, long-term projections of income and expenditure are hard to make with any accuracy. Inflation, the ups and downs of international markets, the fashions and desires of consumers, all interact chaotically. It is, therefore, difficult to draw categorical conclusions from an exercise, such as the projection of the life of a woodland, that goes on over such a long period of time (about 80 years in the case of a birchwood, such as the woodland at Creag Meagaidh) and to translate these conclusions to the circumstances of a private owner. However, the broad message is that there is the real possibility of breaking even over this timescale, and, while a small cash flow deficit cannot be ruled out, nor can a surplus.

A 25-year cash flow forecast was prepared. This showed the costs and income annually for the first ten years, and then the following 15 years in three five-year slices, giving an annual cash flow and cumulative cash flows for the project. Two kinds of cost are included: red deer costs and estate costs. The red deer costs break down into labour (based on the assumption that seven months' worth of estate workers' time is spent on work to do with the control of deer, including monitoring), the red deer cull (the cost of ammunition, the larder and other costs), and red deer 'other' (a heading that includes the annual cost of running an all-terrain vehicle for the removal of deer carcasses from the forest). The estate costs are broken down into staff, estate maintenance, visitor management, depreciation of facilities for visitors and research.

The primary source of income was to be that coming from the WGS. This was to come under two headings: discretionary payments and grants for natural regeneration. The discretionary payment is available for work needed to encourage regeneration. At Creag Meagaidh, deer control was the only work proposed; elsewhere fencing might be included.

Therefore, the net annual cost of qualifying work for grant was estimated at £5650 per year. The establishment of the woodland was assumed to be phased over 25 years. For these purposes, it was assumed that the discretionary payment could be available at the beginning of each five-year WGS period.

The second large item of income would have come from natural regeneration grants. Currently, the grant payable is £525 per hectare, once a minimum stocking rate of 1100 trees per hectare at a height of 30–45 cm is reached. The natural tendency of birch to clump is acceptable to the Forestry Authority and there is no need for even spacing; in fact, varied spacing is a requirement in new native woodlands to emulate natural regeneration.

Annual management grants are available for woodlands of high environmental value, such as those in Creag Meagaidh NNR, for help towards the costs of works to safeguard or enhance the existing environmental value of the woodland, and in particular, to encourage responsible access. They may also be used to improve woodlands that are degraded, but which could be restored. Thirdly, annual management grants may be given to create, maintain or enhance public access to woodlands. On this basis, their availability should be fairly general.

APPENDIX I

Employment costs as fixed or variable costs

Creag Meagaidh differs in one important way from most privately owned deer forests in that the stalking, particularly of stags, has not been let. Owing to the urgent need to reduce the numbers of deer, it was thought essential that stalking should be done by professional stalkers with this sole aim. For stags, the income forgone is about £240 per stag, which, with a sustainable cull of between 20 and 25 stags a year, amounts to between £5000 and £6000 per year. At Mar Lodge, the conditions imposed by the Easter Trust for the gift that enabled the estate to be acquired by the National Trust for Scotland stipulated that the Trust should continue to manage the land as a traditional sporting estate. The cull of red deer at Mar Lodge, therefore, has to continue with paying clients doing some of the shooting, as in the days of private ownership. It will be interesting to see how the cull progresses and how this compares with the experience of the NCC/SNH at Creag Meagaidh. With lower receipts from venison, this potential source of income may need to be reappraised.

Where a landowner's aim is to achieve a large cull to reduce deer numbers or to maximise income from venison, it may be valid to attribute the cost of employing the stalker and ghillie specifically to this task. In accountancy terms, this means treating it as a variable cost. If, on account of the time spent on deer management, the stalker and ghillie are unable to do the other normal estate work, the opportunity cost has also to be considered. In such circumstances (i.e. the treatment of labour costs as variable costs), labour costs may well be higher per beast shot if the stalking is let than if it is not. The stalker and ghillie still have to be there, but the client will shoot no more than a couple of stags in a day, whereas a professional team intent on culling rather than sport may take more animals. In the case of the professional team, where the cost is regarded as variable, every attempt is likely to be made to keep the cost per beast shot as low as possible, including completion of the cull in the shortest possible time to reduce opportunity costs. This may mean that it is better not to have any paying clients in such circumstances, because the financial contribution they make may be smaller than the costs they incur overall.

The main aim of many deer forest owners is to enjoy their forest. The stalker and ghillie are needed for this purpose, so the owner will regard the cost of employing (at least) the stalker as a fixed one, and will be satisfied if income from clients does no more than help defray expenses. In these circumstances, any income generated makes a positive contribution.

APPENDIX J

Stalking and visitors

The possible presence of visitors at all times when stalking is going on means that stalkers have to be carefully trained to be constantly aware of possible danger to other humans. They are expected, increasingly, to undergo safety training courses. SNH's stalkers must have a three-yearly assessment and a certificate of competence. In order to minimise conflict with walkers, SNH's stalkers at Creag Meagaidh try to stalk at dawn as much as possible.

Paul Ramsay graduated from Edinburgh University in social anthropology and went on to study environmental conservation at University College London (MSc 1970). Since then he has had varied experience in farming, estate management and environmental conservation.

An estate owner himself, Paul Ramsay has written and contributed to a number of books on conservation and the landscape of Scotland. Paul and his wife, Louise, and their four children live in North East Perthshire.

Cover photograph by P. & A. MacDonald

ISBN: 1 85397 234 7 (Hardback)
ISBN: 1 85397 238 X (Paperback)

Print code: TH1K1196

Printed on environmentally friendly paper